LEFT, RIGHT & CHRIST

EVANGELICAL FAITH IN POLITICS

LISA SHARON HARPER & D. C. INNES

elevate faith

Published in Boise, Idaho by Elevate Faith,
a division of Elevate Publishing.

Web: www.elevatepub.com

Editorial work by Michelle Rapkin and
AnnaMarie McHargue.

Cover design: Aaron Snethen

Interiors: Aaron Snethen

Library of Congress Control Number: 2016942323

ISBN (print): 9781943425259
ISBN (e-book): 9781943425761

TABLE OF CONTENTS

DEDICATION FROM LISA SHARON HARPER

To my Evangelical brothers and sisters, with love.
There is another way to be true to our faith in the public square.
May we find it. May we walk it. May we live it.
...and may our witness be restored.

Amen.

DEDICATION FROM D.C. INNES

To my dear wife, Jessica, who suffers my shortcomings
and magnifies whatever I have to recommend me.

FOREWORDS

FOREWORD: MARVIN OLASKY

My oldest son is now in his thirties, but in reading *Left, Right & Christ* I flashed back three decades ago to when he was just a toddler. That's when he and I would walk around Wilmington, Delaware playing "the four things game," in which he would tell me the essential difference between three items and one other item. For example, I would point out to him a number on a house, a dog, a trash can, and a baby in a stroller, and then ask, "Which is different?" Such a question, of course, can be sliced and diced in lots of different ways through multi- perspectival analysis, but Pete gave the answer that warmed this daddy's heart: "baby-'cause he's a person."

The game was early SAT preparation, I suppose, but its premise provides a good way to approach this book. For example, I suspect that both David Innes and Lisa Sharon Harper might answer another question about who is different the same way: A persevering missionary, a Christian college professor, a crisis pregnancy center counselor, or Dr. Zarkov of the 1930s Flash Gordon movies. I hope they'd both choose Dr. Zarkov, not only because he's imaginary but because he boasts of his travel on "a rocket ship of my own design." The first three all realize that we travel on a ship of someone else's design and should obey that superior authority.

If Innes and Harper agree that God is in charge, why do they disagree on so many others things? Often it's a matter of perspective. If Innes and Harper played the four things game with the Constitution, Andrew Carnegie's *The Gospel of Wealth*, Karl Marx's *Das Kapital*, and Bill Gates' *The Road Ahead*, I suspect Innes would choose the Constitution, which contains great wisdom because it is grounded in a biblical understanding of human nature. I wouldn't be surprised to see Harper choose *Das Kapital*, on the surmise that the other three all express the views of rich men.

I don't at all doubt Harper's spirituality, and I'm not saying she's a Marxist, but she does have a tendency to concentrate on material circumstances. The divide is perhaps sharpest on abortion. Innes, "pro- life," notes, "When people deny God, they deny life" so a spiritual vacuum leads some sad women to have a doctor vacuum up their tiny babies. Harper, also pro-life, focuses on the material: "Lives are saved when we address abortion for what it is, a poverty issue." If that were true, we would have had in the 19th and early 20th centuries, when Americans on average were much poorer than we are now, many more abortions in proportion to the population than we currently do. But we did not. In African and South American countries much poorer than ours, the abortion rate is much lower, at least until radical feminists from America arrive and proclaim a gospel of death. No, lives are saved when we address abortion for what it is, man's forgetting that we are traveling on a rocket ship of God's design.

On some issues, like abortion, God's will is clear. On others, like how to reform health care, it's not. Innes and Harper both identify problems in our current system and propose different solutions. If Innes played the four things game with food, shelter, breathing, and doctors' visits, I suspect he'd conclude that breathing is the exception because it doesn't cost anything (at least when our lungs work and the air is not polluted). Innes argues for a market system in which health care providers compete for our patronage. Harper, though, ends her essay with a "call for universal care that protects and cultivates the image of God in all Americans." A good sentiment, but why not also call for government to provide universal food and shelter?

We haven't done that because we know the market system works best for at least 90 percent of the people; we can then concentrate on providing food and shelter only for those unable to provide for themselves. The same approach would work in health care: instead of messing with a system that, with occasional exceptions, serves reasonably well (given this fallen world) at least 90 percent of Americans, why not step in only for those in need by expanding and bulwarking the network of free or low-cost community clinics that already exists, and making sure that Medicare and Medicaid are funded for the major health problems.

Here's where we come to a decisive difference between the political left and the political right: the left emphasizes equality; the right emphasizes liberty. Either position taken too far becomes an idol; as New York pastor Tim Keller notes, "Idolatry is taking a good thing and making it an ultimate thing." But one problem with an equality emphasis that may look good in the abstract is that in practice it requires a big government. History shows that centers of power attract power-seekers who then attract money-seekers, and the result is a new ruling class: In a fallen world "equality" is an ever-receding horizon.

I suspect that both writers and my brother, Jim, understand that if we aren't Christians first, second, and third, we're idol worshippers. But it's disingenuous to suggest that Christian citizens, united in a devotion to Christ, can or should avoid questions of political philosophy. We should be willing to declare our positions on the horizontal spectrum. On issue after issue, we have to make decisions and vote, or else we abdicate. So I appreciate the honest acknowledgment at the core of this book that Harper is on the left and Innes is on the right.

This is different from being a partisan who claims that either Democrats or Republicans always have the right answers. In WORLD, for example, we criticized the Bush administration at times, and we've often criticized conservatives who violated the trust of their spouses and the public. As Christians, we know that all people are fallen sinners, and we all often get things wrong. Most Evangelicals also know both from the Bible and from history that concentrations of political power lead to oppression, and that's why American Evangelicals overwhelmingly favor limited government and political decentralization. That's what it means to be on the right, and to oppose both international and national socialism.

That's why I'll say that theologically and politically we should have no king but Jesus.

This book is worth reading because both Harper and Innes are unafraid to state their positions, issue by issue, and acknowledge how those positions connect. But instead of proceeding chapter by chapter, I'll commend to you now this entire book, which has nuggets throughout and many points to dispute. If this isn't a discussion starter for Christians, nothing else will be.

FOREWORD: JIM WALLIS

"Left" and "Right" are political categories. They are not religious terms. And when religion tries to fit into political categories; religion gets distorted—always. So what we have is politicized religion. But what we need is prophetic faith—the kind of faith that can challenge politics, that can confront both left and right. But there is little of that these days. Instead there is more religious cheerleading for partisan politics—on both sides.

I have sometimes said, "Don't go left, don't go right, go deeper." And that statement really annoys Marvin Olasky, who writes the other foreword to this book. He has pressured me to just call myself "a man of the left" like he calls himself "a man of the right." He may want to identify himself that way. But I won't do it—ever. And, frankly, I don't think he should either. Since we are both Christians, we should have the capacity to challenge the left and the right; when they are wrong. And they both are sometimes, even many times, just wrong.

To state the obvious: We should be Christians first; and everything else second, third, fourth, or whatever. I really believe that. And the word "Christian" should be the defining term in any phrase about our identity, i.e. we really shouldn't be the "religious right" or the "religious left." We should be Christians first and foremost; and neither political party or ideological side should rest easy where we are concerned. They should never be able to take us for granted, never count us as a reliable part of their base, and never just turn to us to be their chaplains or cheerleaders. We should rather make politicians and politics always nervous, and worried that, at any time, we are going to say, like the biblical prophets often did, "Thus says the Lord," or "Woe unto you," or even "You are the man!"

Can politicians be counted upon to always protect the dignity of life? No, instead both parties show that some lives are more important to them than others in a very selective political morality. Can the politicians be relied upon to protect the poor and vulnerable as the Scriptures command? No, they will always prefer those who vote and donate to their election campaigns than those who don't or can't. The Republicans consistently defend the interests of the upper class, and the Democrats always appeal for the votes of the middle class. Neither sees it as their primary task to defend the poor; but God tells us that's our vocation as people of faith. Jesus did not say in the 25th chapter of Matthew, "As you have done to the rich or middle class, you have done to me." He said we would be judged by how we treated "the least of these." I can testify that when you say that in the White House or at the Congress, it really makes them nervous. Both of our political parties have failed that test. Can the politicians be trusted to pursue peace, or even restrict war to the last resort? No, because war is such a good financial and political business.

But are their prudential choices to make in politics, can voting make a difference, and are some policy choices better than others. Yes, of course, and this book is about those choices. But even there, it is better that the choices Christians make don't always follow politically partisan lines. God is emphatically not a Republican or a Democrat.

Lisa Sharon Harper and D.C. Innes have written a book that takes up these questions, and they engage in a far-ranging dialogue about many issues of public policy. Obviously, you won't agree with everything each author has to say, I didn't, but you will find the discussion quite stimulating—which is clearly the purpose of the book. Clearly, I agree more with Lisa Sharon Harper and Olasky with D.C. Innes, hence the two forewords.

I will let you read them both and decide for yourself where you stand on all these policy issues. But I will say a couple things about the difference in the two authors' approaches.

D.C. Innes is a Canadian become an American; as my father was. But I must say that his complete and almost worshipful embrace of American individualism troubles me as a Christian. At times in this book, Innes sounds much more like Ayn Rand, the Russian atheist and apostle of the virtues of selfishness, than he does Jesus Christ. As Rand herself bluntly states, her extolling of selfish individualism is in direct contrast with the teachings and example of Christ. You have to choose between the two, and can't have both as Innes tries to do.

Lisa Sharon Harper, on the other hand, strongly embraces personal responsibility, but also lifts up the vision of the common good and the biblical call for social justice. She knows when we only focus on ourselves, or our government only focuses on protecting the property rights of those who already have property, for example, we lose something very important. My Canadian immigrant dad was a World War II Navy veteran, mechanical engineer, successful businessman, church founding pastor, and father of five children; so he knew the meaning of personal responsibility. But his life, his faith, and his idea of both citizenship and government didn't end there. He was always asking about the well-being of the wider community, about all the workers at Detroit Edison, about his city of Detroit, about the racial and economic fairness and equity of his country, and about the values expressed by America in the world. And he would have hated Ayn Rand.

I found D.C. Innes often setting up false choices and unnecessary absolutes. Liberalism is all and always bad; conservatism is all and always good etc. And his incessant warnings about a post-modern statism that wants "control of all things" seems more than a little overblown. He says he's against the government even trying to good things for people's lives. "If it were government's responsibility, even in part, to do the good deeds of society, people would gradually surrender more and more of private responsibility to it. For its part, government would gradually expand to take responsibility for everything it possibly could. It would soon have agencies tying your shoes, blowing your nose, and tucking you in at night." Really? And who is it that wants that?

As somebody who has always strongly advocated for faith-based and other organizations in a vibrant civil society taking real leadership in solving social problems, in *partnership* with both the public and private sectors; Innes's choices seem extreme to me. Nobody did better, for example, in their response to Hurricane Katrina than the faith community, but we can't build levies or provide health care for all who need it. A better way is for each sector to do what they do best and, sometimes, what they only can do. But there is little middle way for Innes: Nanny state totalitarianism or the wilderness of unregulated corporate capitalism, moderated only by the church's private charity.

Lisa Sharon Harper is more pragmatic than Innes. She doesn't put her hope in either government or the market; but in the church's vision of the Kingdom of God and the faith-inspired movements for social change it can help to spark and spawn. But she also knows the practical impact, especially on the poorest and most vulnerable, of public policies that can either help or hurt real people. It can, as she points out, stop or allow "lynching, school segregation, and employment discrimination." And Lisa's personal perspective is very different from Innes. She says, "Policies either helped my family flourish or limited its liberty to the point of oppression...As a woman of African, Native American, Puerto Rican, Caribbean, Jewish, and Anglo descent, I am profoundly aware of the power of policy, systems, structures, and institutions to oppress or liberate whole people groups."

And by the way Marvin, I hear Lisa talk about Scripture all the time, but have never heard her mention *Das Kapital.* C'mon. And she is as pro-life as anyone I know. It's just that she actually wants to reduce abortion in the world, hence the concern about supporting low- income women who have the majority of abortions, instead of just talking symbolically about the issue.

So read for yourself, and see what you think. But remember the limitations and temptations of politics. And that if you try to fit your faith into political categories, your faith will simply lose its proper shape.

PUBLISHER'S PREFACE

Growing up, I frequently heard the refrain that we should not discuss religion or politics in public. The topics, on their own, were too divisive, I suppose. And if you couldn't speak of them separately, discussing them together would be even more dangerous, indeed a powder keg waiting to explode.

Through the years, however, I have become convinced that we need to think and converse about religion and politics, particularly their relationship to one another.

Both are topics way too important to be ignored. But we also need a good way to go about dialoguing on these subjects. As one who has spent years of my life in churches and communities on both side of the theological and political aisle, I've experienced, firsthand, the misunderstandings that can arise between the various viewpoints.

All too often, I've heard people dismiss the "other side" because they didn't understand where "their side" was coming from. I've also seen debates become fruitless as people emotionally dig in their heels. It's no wonder we were advised not to discuss these topics in public. More often than not, feelings are hurt and bridges are burned.

The goal of this book is to find a new way.

The beauty of *Left, Right & Christ* is that, unlike televised debates where both sides can interrupt and break up thought processes, in a book, the authors have an allotted space to really make their case. No interruptions are allowed. The same principle applies to the reader. We can't cut the author off like we can in conversation.

We need a safe conversation space for these topics and this book is that space.

And in this book we have two strong leaders to guide the conversation. Several years ago, I interviewed Lisa Sharon Harper for *The Other Journal*. I had the phone on speaker and my wife overheard the interview. When I was done, Laurie said exactly what I was thinking, "That lady is a genius."

A while later, I met with Marvin Olasky and told him about my idea for this book and how I'd like to have Lisa paired with an equally smart and competent Christian leader who has thought thoroughly on these topics. He connected me with D.C. Innes and I'm glad he did. D.C. has a keen intellect and a sharp wit and has out-thought most people in the world on the relationship of faith and politics.

I consider both authors genuine friends and I'm honored to work with them. Their word is not the final word. We all need to continue conversing on these topics. But their word is a good word and I hope you take it seriously.

MARK L. RUSSELL

PART 1

INTRODUCTIONS

OUR SEPARATE JOURNEYS

OUR SEPARATE JOURNEYS

D.C. INNES

After 9/11, many ex-pat Canadians, like ABC anchor Peter Jennings and White House speech writer David Frum, applied for citizenship, fully embracing what they had taken for granted but could suddenly see was precious to them. As for me, my green card was still in process when the twin towers fell. Three months later, I sat in the Immigration and Naturalization Service office in Des Moines waiting for my green card interview. On the TV monitor, a newly released video showed Osama bin Laden rejoicing as he watched his hellish plans unfold on television. Just as he was striking a stinging blow against our country, there on the monitor, I was deepening in my commitment to it, legally and emotionally.

My affection and high respect for America went much further back than 9/11, back to my arrival here in 1985. Though I originally came here only for graduate studies, I knew from the start that this was no ordinary country. I remember riding "the T" along Commonwealth Avenue in Boston, thinking, "Wow. This is where it all happened. These are Americans, the people who transformed the world."

Occasionally, an American classmate would ask me why a Canadian would want to study American government. I would ask them in turn why a Gaul would want to study politics in Rome, or a why a Dane would cross the channel to study British government. The United States is one of the great civilizations of the world. It is the great guarantor and hope of liberty in the world, over against the constant encroachment of tyranny (Iran, Russia, North Korea, Venezuela, etc.). I have always appreciated this, even as an undergraduate in Toronto.

This respect for America as a country of noble liberty, of surprising innovation, and of unapologetic, world-transforming energy made the Republican Party, where those sentiments are the norm, a natural political home for me.

* * *

I was not born in a Republican household. I didn't grow up with Republican table talk. I came into alignment with the Republican Party not from the Democratic Party, nor from a more radical stream of American politics, nor from a position of apolitical indifference. In fact, my political beginnings were from outside the country entirely. My parents are highland Scots, and I was born and raised in Toronto, Canada.

I have always been conservative. It was a matter of temperament. But it was also part of being Canadian, though we don't often think of Canadians as reflexive conservatives. Orderliness and obedience to law are characteristically Canadian. Perhaps it is the influence of climate or Scottish Presbyterianism or perhaps the convictions of the United Empire Loyalists who formed English Canada when they fled the rebellious American colonies. Whatever the reason, a Canadian will stop at a red light at 3 a.m. at a deserted intersection and remain there until the light changes.

As school children, we were told that whereas in America it was the settlers who first ventured into the frontier, followed by the railroad, and only then the law, in Canada it was just the opposite. First went the Mounties, then the railroads, and only then the settlers. I cannot say how true that is historically, but the point it was intended to illustrate is certainly true. Canadians are an obedient lot.

Our teachers also reminded us that whereas the American principles of government are "life, liberty, and the pursuit of happiness," Canada is founded on the principles of "peace, order, and good government." But I later came to realize that, while peace and order are indispensible political goods, that motto opens the door to suffocating government action and a frightening disappearance of personal responsibility when "good government" comes to mean central control of all things. After my move south from Canada, my growing concern over this trend in modern politics steered me sharply into the Republican Party where people share this concern.

I always believed government to be good. The mayhem that the nation observed with horror during the Halifax police strike of 1981 was sufficient argument that without some kind of forceful and effective government, life is miserable and short. It was only after I became a Christian and recognized God's authority behind it and His blessing in it that I fully understood that goodness.

But I also sensed that government has a limited function and place. For example, it was clear to me that the Soviet Union was government completely out of control (though a disturbing multitude of leftist fellow citizens, especially in the university system, couldn't see that). A more benign example, but nonetheless real to me, was Pierre Trudeau's Liberal government, my own government at the time. The Liberals were in power from before I could walk until just before I graduated from university.[1] As I came of age politically, I developed an appreciation for why bossy, know-it-all government, though strong on "peace" and "order," is far from "good." Looking south at America, I could see that the people who shared my appreciation were largely in one party: the Republican Party.

Whereas in the United States, the most enduring and troubling point of division has been race, in Canada it has always been language: the English-French divide. From its colonial beginnings as Upper and Lower Canada after the American Revolution, Canada has been two nations, even after Confederation in 1867. Part of Trudeau's remedy for this problem, which had broken out into violent separatist unrest in the 1960s, was to make the French feel at home in the whole country by forcing the French language on English Canada, the nine provinces other than Quebec.

My opposition to this was not a matter of dislike for the French language itself, which is like music when well-spoken. Neither was I concerned about individual choice in the matter. My concern was community centered. Toronto was not a French-speaking city, and still isn't. The government, in my view, was being heavy handed and presumptuous in attempting to remedy the French separatist threat by forcing communities in English Canada to become something they did not want to be and which was alien to their way of life: bilingual.

The Trudeau language policy followed a modern liberal impulse. I am speaking here of "liberal" in the classical, Enlightenment sense of the word. It abstracts from actual human beings and their relationships and treats them as interchangeable human-being-units, as it were. Liberal governments that take their liberalism seriously, as Pierre Trudeau did, attempt to homogenize society, making it more rational, like math, and thus to render people more efficiently governable.

Liberal government is modern scientific government. It works through an administrative state that governs as much as possible from the center by technocrats—unelected, technically-trained bureaucrats. This was and still is the Liberal Party of Canada. As scientific and technocratic, it is therefore post-partisan and trans-political. I still view this approach to government as political poison. It robs people of precisely what it misguidedly tries to secure for them: their human dignity. In America, it finds its home in the Democratic Party.

Trudeau hated Canada's British past and, with equal passion, our American neighbor. Starting in my teen years, both of these set me at odds with him and with whatever political orientation inspired him. My time in graduate school at Boston College gave me the distance to see that the British connection was a lost fight, but also that America was a cause well worth a fight to preserve.

Canada was British North America. That is, it was neither Britain nor America, but the British political tradition of responsible government transplanted into, and at the same time transformed by, the North American context. To reject the country's British associations was to reject the country's great and defining heritage in favor of a dubious and ill-conceived experiment.

I eventually came to see that the Canada I thought still existed in some remnant form or might one day again exist had long ago passed away and was never returning.[2] Under the Liberal prime minister who governed my boyhood, the maple leaf flag, a banner without any obvious historical content, replaced the old Red Ensign.

As I was passing into young adulthood, Dominion Day changed to Canada Day, an empty name for a meaningless day. It didn't instruct the citizen in any way, but I suspect that was the point. Celebrate Canada, and give that word whatever meaning you choose. There was certainly no reference to the Fathers of Confederation, their hopes for the country, and the heritage that had come down to us, regardless of our ethnic background, from the British parliamentary tradition.

Finally, in 1982, Trudeau "patriated" the Canadian Constitution. The British North America Act, an act of British Parliament, had served as Canada's constitution since the North American colonies confederated in 1867. After lengthy negotiations with the provincial governments, the Trudeau government replaced it with the Constitution Act. This buried the old order. But by that time it had long ago crumbled into dust, and its unrecognizable ruins were many layers beneath a new civilization.

Strong anti-Americanism was prominent in Trudeau's thinking and policies (whereas he was quite chummy with Cuba's Fidel Castro). Ironically, however, it was Trudeau who succeeded in giving Canada a Charter of Rights and Freedoms, bundled with the new constitution, an innovation that introduced an American element into the Canadian political tradition and promoted a more American way of thinking.[3] Most Canadians have some anti-American leanings, and in my distaste for American individualism, I was no different.

John Diefenbaker, prime minister from 1957-1963, was the first to introduce Canada to the idea of a bill of rights.[4] For this reason, I viewed him with great suspicion. To me, individual rights meant selfish people shattering their community's way of life by asserting their right to be in it but unaffected by it, and by denying communities the right to live the life of a community with its religious and moral traditions. The notion of a charter of rights rubbed my Tory fur the wrong way.

I opposed gun rights, for example, and in this I was not unusual, even for a conservative Canadian. Nor did I give property rights anywhere near the value that I do today. I thought that if the community believes your ownership of certain property is incompatible with the good of the community or perhaps even your use of it in a particular way, community good must trump private property. After all, it is only because of one's membership in the community that one can have any security and even prosperity in one's property. I viewed the whole notion of individual rights, and the narrow self-centeredness that it encourages, as destructive to the relationships that make up the fabric of human life—family, friends, community—and on which most human good depends.

Though I was no Yankophile, I was nonetheless certain that the United States was a model vastly to be preferred over the Soviet Communists, union-strangled Britain, and the politically enfeebled Europeans. As an adult, viewing my country from south of the border, I saw government power expanding without check and, at the federal level, centralizing in the Prime Minister's Office.

There was no principle aside from fiscal sanity that one could invoke to stop this trend. Politically, I saw a reflexive preference for government action, often in the name of cultivating national unity. Or the appeal would be to the principle of equality understood as equality of condition or equal outcomes, but there was no tradition of prizing individual liberty to temper that appeal. In 2008, someone asked Dean Steacy, the principal investigator for Canadian Human Rights Commission in hate crime cases, "What value do you give freedom of speech when you investigate?" He replied, "Freedom of speech is an American concept, so I don't give it any value."[5]

In America, a great battle rages. On the one side are the defenders of liberty as understood by the Founders and as bequeathed to us in our great founding documents, the Declaration of Independence and the Constitution. On the other side are the advocates of post-modern, progressive statism. There is no such battle in Canada. North of our border there is only the political correctness of the left, and everything else is thoughtcrime. If anyone expresses any doubt about the liberal social agenda, he is labeled a Nazi and other standard epithets.

The two major American political parties take their respective stands on one side and the other of this battle, the Republicans for the Founding and the Democrats for the Progressive rejection of it. That's why I am a Republican.

My conversion to Christ marked a decisive step in the journey from my Canadian Toryism to my American republicanism. I don't mean to question the faith or spiritual maturity of Christians who are Canadian Tories. I am only saying that the Christian view of man prompted me to move toward the modern republican view of politics as the most prudent way for fallen people to live with one another politically.

Trusting in men, that is, in the good character of one's neighbors and rulers, seemed to me a noble, salutary way of life for a community. When my high school installed a security system by the library checkout desk and placed metal security strips in all the books, I was disgruntled. I knew there were library books disappearing from the collection, but I saw the choice of a technological solution, instead of a moral one, as giving up on the effort to prevent stealing by developing good character in the students.

Society, I believed, depends on virtue generally distributed in the populace, and particularly featured in political leadership. Of course there is vice and so people steal library books. But by relying on a technological fix we simply resign ourselves to our vice, assume it, and outsmart it. Of course, I wasn't against locks and a police force.

I still see the cultivation of good character in people as essential to a healthy society and good political order. It maintains moral laws, strong families, and flourishing religion. These all cultivate an expectation across the culture that everyone should act with decency toward one another.

Since coming to a saving understanding of the gospel, however, I have been working through its implications for politics. That begins with a deeper appreciation for the implications of human depravity—the effect that sin has even on the best of us, but especially as it shows itself in the worst of us. In *The Federalist Papers* no. 51, James Madison wrote, "If men were angels, no government would be necessary."

People are less than angelic—even, at times, demonic—and for this reason a wise people structures its government in a way that takes account of this in human beings, not only in the ruled but also in the rulers. This way, they take appropriate measures to ensure, so far as possible, that government actually does its job.

Most governments have only the appearance of government, but in substance they are what Augustine calls "great robberies." A well- structured constitution anticipates that problem, and the American Constitution is marvelously well-structured.

Strangely enough, it was my close encounter with the Enlightenment political theory of John Locke (1632-1704) that brought me to see the superior virtues of the American Constitution, and thus to affiliate with the party that I think takes it more seriously. I say "strangely enough" because Enlightenment philosophy is arguably at odds with the Bible. Nonetheless, I came to see that, as a tradition that sought to establish government based not on the way men ought to behave but on how they do behave, or at least can in most circumstances be expected to behave, it took better account of sinful human character than the older political traditions did.

For the last fifty years and into the foreseeable future, Canada has three, and only three, models from which to choose for its identity: America North, British North America, or post-modern Euro-North America. Led by its left-wing intellectuals, Canada has chosen the Euro-model, and so is following (though not mirroring) Europe in its economic, moral, spiritual, and demographic problems. Given that, I have chosen America. And I find the Republican Party is fighting to preserve that uniquely American model as the Democrats steer us toward Europe.

LISA SHARON HARPER

Politics is one of two things for most of us. For some, it is a high-level battle of ideas fueled by ideology, philosophy and sometimes theology. For others, politics is about public policies that shape the flow of life on the ground, it is personal. For me it is the latter.

My ancestors' stories laid the foundation for my story. Ours is an American story. Evident throughout my family tree are the twisted scars left by the shaping forces of public policy that bent ancestral branches in one direction or another.

My grandfather's branch, Cherokee and Chickasaw Native Americans, yielded to the power of public policy when the Indian Removal Act of 1930 ordered the forced removal of the five tribes from southeastern homelands they had known for thousands of years. The Act removed them because gold was found on their land. My ancestors escaped in the middle of the tearful walk that took the rest of their people 800 miles away to Oklahoma—Indian Territory. Sixteen thousand Cherokees walked the Trail of Tears in the middle of winter. Four thousand died. My ancestors lived the consequences of public policies born of greed and watched those policies kill thousands of men, women, and children as they walked westward in bloody snow.

My grandmother's branch, Africans who had been brought to America, bore the brunt of public policies passed in Virginia in the seventeenth century. Lea Ballard was born in Kershaw County, South Carolina in 1836. Her mother was an enslaved woman. Lea was classified as "mulatto" (half black and half white) on the 1880 census. We don't know who her father was, but we know he was white. Judicial law established in 1640 and 1662 determined the course of Lea's life.[6] According to the law, even though Lea was half white, she was enslaved upon birth because her mother was a slave. Of Lea's 13 children (from five husbands who were sold away or died), those born before the Emancipation Proclamation were born into perpetual slavery, because Lea was a slave. Lea was my great great great grandmother.

My birth father's paternal grandparents, Reginald Weeks and Anita Weeks Richarson, immigrated to the United States from the U.S. Commonwealth of Puerto Rico in 1913. In 1917, the Jones Act granted the people of Puerto Rico limited U.S. citizenship, making it possible for great grandpa Weeks to bring his family to the states. By 1930, the entire Weeks family was settled in the South Bronx, New York City.

My father, Dennis, was a member of the New York City chapter of C.O.R.E. (Congress of Racial Equality) in 1964. He almost joined the '64 Freedom Summer Project with fellow New Yorkers Michael "Mickey"

Schwerner and Andrew Goodman, but he decided to stay back in the city to work a summer job instead. Soon after Schwerner and Goodman arrived in Mississippi to help register black Mississippians to vote, they were assigned to accompany James Cheney, a local black C.O.R.E. member, to check in on members of a church that had recently been burned down in Neshoba County, Mississippi. On the morning of June 21, 1964 the three men set out for Neshoba County. That evening, on their way back, they were chased by two carloads of Ku Klux Klan members who shot them dead one by one and buried them in an earthen dam. The deaths of Schwerner, Goodman and Cheney turned the focus of all Americans on the brutal reality of southern segregation and paved the way for passage of the Voting Rights Act of 1965.

Up to this point, the American political landscape was not so starkly divided down ideological lines. Conservatives and progressives found their home in both the Democratic and Republican Parties. The great divide was triggered by the Democrats' passage of the Civil Rights Act of 1964 and the Voting Rights Act of 1965.

Throughout the 1940s, Southern Democrats vehemently fought civil rights activists' and northern Democrats' efforts to pass anti-lynching and anti-poll tax laws through the U.S. Congress. Into this context—a Democratic Party paralyzed by multi-interest malaise—Minneapolis Mayor Hubert Humphrey took the stage at the '48 Democratic National Committee Convention to speak on behalf of the Minority Report on Civil Rights.[9]

Humphrey said, "It seems to me that the Democratic Party needs to make definite pledges of the kind suggested in the Minority Report to maintain the trust and the confidence placed in it by the people of all races in all sections of this country." And, he said, "For those who say that we are rushing this issue of civil rights, I say to them, 'We are 172 years late!'" He continued, "For those who say this civil rights program is an infringement on states' rights, I say this: 'The time has arrived in America for the

Democratic Party to get out of the shadows of states' rights and to walk forthrightly into the bright sunshine of human rights!'"[10]

Upon a vote, the pro-civil rights plank was adopted as part of the DNC platform for the 1948 election season. It called for federal legislation to combat lynching, school segregation, and employment discrimination.

Thirty-five delegates from Mississippi and Alabama staged a walk out of the Convention. They formed the Dixiecrat Party (aka The States Rights Democratic Party) and nominated South Carolina Governor Strom Thurmond as its presidential candidate; his platform opposed racial integration and called for the preservation of Jim Crow laws and white supremacy.[11] The party was short-lived, and by 1950 most Dixiecrats were absorbed back into the Democratic Party. Then Democratic President Lyndon B. Johnson's Congress passed the Civil Rights Act of 1964 and Voting Rights Act of 1965. Dixiecrats defected the Democratic Party en masse and found their new home in the heart of the Republican Party. They have been there ever since.

Public policies shaped the course of family life on every limb of my family tree. Policies either helped my family flourish or limited its liberty to the point of oppression. As a result, I grew up with a strong sense of the private value of public political engagement.

So, it felt natural to walk from row house to row house, up and down Walnut Lane in the West Oak Lane neighborhood of Philadelphia, Pennsylvania with my mother in the fall of 1976. Sometimes mom knocked. Sometimes I did. Curious mothers, grandmothers, fathers, children—most of whom we knew—opened doors and my mom launched into her spiel: "Have you registered to vote?" she asked.

Back in the mid-1960s Mom was a founding member of the Philadelphia chapter of S.N.C.C. (Student Non-violent Coordinating Committee). Now, a decade later, she was the judge of elections for her neighborhood in Philadelphia and was active in getting out the vote. On this day, as mom held my seven-year-old hand, walking from house to house, I began to wonder: "Why are we Democrats?" I knew we were for Jimmy Carter. There were "Jimmy Carter for President" signs in our front lawn and Mom and Dad loved to talk about how great he would be for the country. But I didn't get it. Why not Ford? He was already President. It would be easier just to stick with him. He didn't look like a bad guy. So, as we approached a new house I asked: "Mom, why are we Democrats?"

In the space between the sidewalk and the front door, Mom explained: "Jimmy Carter is a Democrat. President Ford is a Republican. The Democrats are like Robin Hood; they take back money from the rich and give it to the poor. The Republicans steal money from the poor and give it to the rich. That's why we're Democrats."

It was good enough for me. I loved Robin Hood, so I would be a Democrat, too.

And I was a happy Democrat until I became a born again Christian seven years later in August 1983, at a Sunday evening camp church meeting in Cape May, New Jersey. It was the start of Ronald Reagan's run for his second term in office when a devout friend in my youth group told me very soon after I prayed the prayer of salvation that I would need to be born again...again (so-to-speak). Though I wasn't of voting age, I would have to become a Republican if I was going to call myself a Christian.

I was a true believer, so I began to trumpet the triumphant values of Reaganomics and the trickle-down theory to my mother, who looked at me like I was an alien from outer space. She countered with stories that revealed just how much—or little—was actually trickling down. She explained that Reagan cut vegetables from public school lunches. "Many children depend on these lunches for the only meal they have in a day," she said. "And Reagan actually tried to count catsup as a vegetable."

I met my first Evangelical Democrats in the Church of the Nazarene in New York City in late 1990. I was fascinated. I almost wanted to reach out and touch them to make sure they weren't some kind of mirage. When I moved to Los Angeles in 1991, to attend the Bresee Institute for Urban Mission, I learned a quote attributed to Phineas F. Bresee: "There is no holiness without social holiness."

Bresee founded the very first Church of the Nazarene on skid row in downtown Los Angeles in 1895. Now, in 1991, this Evangelical church was dedicated to doing justice in the city. Sitting side by side in old wooden pews, both Democrats and Republicans worshipped the same Jesus on Sunday mornings. They called on both of their parties to exercise a prophetic kind of leadership, the kind that protects and cultivates the image of God on earth.

It was during my year at the Bresee Institute that I realized two things: 1) I don't have to betray the cries of my ancestors and the current plight of my people to be a follower of Jesus. In fact, by closing my eyes to the impact of conservative policies on my own family, I would fail to see that Jesus walked with my family and my ancestors. He understands. It is okay for me to be a Democrat; and 2) indiscriminate allegiance to any political party is idolatry and to practice idolatry is to become an enemy of God.[12]

Thus, I offer these reflections, not as an apologetic for my political party from a Christian point of view. Rather, these are my reflections on the issues of our times and where both parties stand from the vantage point of my Evangelical faith.

My ancestors' status as ethnic minorities and immigrants in the United States offered them the unique experience of both contributing much to and being profoundly shaped by the American public square. While they lived and loved and worked in the context of families and communities and relationships, the grand trajectories of their lives were often shaped by the overwhelming force of public policies enacted in their times. Sometimes those policies blessed. Sometimes they cursed.

Jesus said in Matthew 25, "When you did it to the least of these, who are my family, you did it to me." Jesus identifies with the oppressed. He identifies with the ones who live their lives on the margins. And He calls them His family.

In our American democracy we the people are the government. So, not only will we the people be judged by the annuls of history according to how we treated the least, but we the people—all of us—will ultimately stand before God. We the people will be called to account for the effect of our public policies on the least of these in our society. Did we bless or did we curse?

Blessing or cursing; that is our choice. [13]

OUR COMMON GROUND

OUR COMMON GROUND

Christians are people whom the Lord by his grace has redeemed out of bondage to sin. Our chief love is Jesus, and his Word is our rule.

Both of us are Christians. And so what we have in common is greater than all our differences. Yet differences there are, and in this book we elaborate on our political differences, in particular. How can two people who share the same fundamental Christian principles—profound, life-transforming, world-transforming principles—differ as sharply as we do at times on something that is also profoundly important like politics? Perhaps that is a question for readers to figure out.

* * *

We begin together in the first chapter of Genesis. God made the heavens and the earth and all that is in them (Gen. 1:1). This world belongs to Him, He rules it, and we take our directions from Him in how we live in it. From the start we know that we enjoy a special relationship not only to God above but also to the world around us. He made us "in His image" (Gen. 1:26). He made us to represent Him in the created world, bearing the stamp of His righteous character, called to govern in His righteous will. So in virtually the same breath, He tells us to "take dominion over the earth," to fill it and rule it (Gen. 1:28).

Being made in God's image entails a responsibility for the creation, as well as a responsibility for one another. People as image-bearers have an inherent dignity and value, and so our relationship with each other should always be one of love. As Christians we are called to love God and love our neighbor—the two great commandments—on every level of our existence: personal, interpersonal, social, and political.

For this reason, the Bible emphasizes the moral responsibility of people, especially the people of God, to care for the poor among them, including the widow and the orphan. These are people whose humanity as image-bearers we find especially easy to forget. The prophets carry words of judgment for those who praise the Lord with their mouths but oppress the weak with their hands. Outsiders like migrants, travelers, and temporary residents suffer the same kind of discrimination, and so receive a special word of concern from the God who hears.

As God made us loving beings, i.e., made to love Him with all our heart, soul, mind, and strength and to love one another as ourselves, He thus made us political beings (Mark 12:30.). We were made to live in community with one another, even as God himself—one God in three persons—is a divine Trinitarian community existing in perfect love (1 John 4:8).

We learn from this that government is vitally important and politics is fundamentally good. God established it for His good purposes (Rom. 13:1-6). That human community, life together under God in the bond of love, is the Kingdom of God (Acts 28:31).

Because of the fall, sin has shattered that perfect bond, thrown off that sweet lordship, and turned the Kingdom into a rebellion of cosmic proportions. Since the cross and the empty tomb, however, Jesus Christ has been spreading his Kingdom and re-creating the world in love. His redemptive power not only saves people for heaven but also restores them for every relationship in this world: with God in worship, with one another in friendship, mercy, service, and obedience, and with the earth in godly stewardship.

But that spreading Kingdom is, as theologians say, already and not yet. It has come and it is yet to come. So while Christ's redemptive work is in process, life is not fully as it should be, and political life is no exception. In a fallen world, political power, though given by God for our good, is seductive. It wants to be everything, and as such can become idolatrous.

The Kingdom of God is not the kingdom of man. It comes by the work of God by grace, spiritually. It does not come by human means, politically and economically. Nonetheless, the Kingdom of God has revolutionary implications for political and economic activity.

The Bible presents our relationship with the world in terms of both distance and engagement. In a sense, God calls us to be separate. We are sojourners in the world, pilgrims passing through and looking for a better country, a heavenly one (Heb. 11:16). This world is not our home. Rather, our citizenship is in heaven (Php. 3:20).

But that holy distance leaves us with greater responsibility in this world than we had before we knew the Lord, because to whom much is given, much is required (Luke 12:48). It is not the distance of disengagement. We live in a democratic republic where, as Lincoln said, government is of the people, by the people, and for the people, so political disengagement is not a moral option. Nor is it an option for Christians who act faithfully as salt and light in the world.

As exiles in a spiritually foreign land, our model for life in this world is the Israelites in their Babylonian exile. God's instruction to them was to be a blessing not only to one another, but also to their pagan neighbors and to the place where God had planted them (Jer. 29:4-7):

This is what the LORD Almighty, the God of Israel, says to all those I carried into exile from Jerusalem to Babylon: "Build houses and settle down; plant gardens and eat what they produce. Marry and have sons and daughters; find wives for your sons and give your daughters in marriage, so that they too may have sons and daughters. Increase in number there; do not decrease. Also, seek the peace and prosperity of the city to which I have carried you into exile. Pray to the LORD for it, because if it prospers, you too will prosper.

So, while the Lord tarries, Christians in America are to prosper our country, help make it a better place in every respect: more just, more equitable, more merciful, more wise, more beautiful, more fruitful, more flourishing in every way that God desires human communities to flourish. As we have the mind of Christ through whom the world was made, Christians should stand out in our understanding of what that flourishing looks like and how to get there. This book is our debate between the political left and right over what that understanding is.

PART 2

FOUNDATIONS

LIBERTY AND JUSTICE

ON THE ROLE OF GOVERNMENT

ON THE ROLE OF GOVERNMENT

LISA SHARON HARPER

The American ideal of "Liberty and Justice for all" reminds me of the first time I voted. I stood in line at a Rutgers University frat house in New Brunswick, New Jersey; it was 1988. Vice President George H. W. Bush was vying for the top spot against challenger Michael Dukakis. With each step closer to the voting booth, I wiped tears from my face. I was proud to live in a country where the rule of the land is one person, one vote. I was overwhelmed because I knew I was reaping the fruit of the labor of the women and men who established our nation's credo: "with liberty and justice for all."

I owed my ability to register as a Democrat or Republican to the men and women who participated in our revolution and the Civil War. I owed my right to pull the lever to the women who suffered through imprisonment and hunger strikes to win the right to vote. Finally, I owed my right to equal protection of these rights to the non-violent warriors who walked holes into their shoes and offered their bodies as living sacrifices to establish a more perfect union through the Civil Rights Movement. I stood in line to vote and I was grateful. I am grateful.

Perhaps the greatest articulation of this ideal is found in the Preamble to the Declaration of Independence, penned by Thomas Jefferson: "We hold these truths to be self-evident, that all men are created equal, that they are endowed by their Creator with certain unalienable rights, that among these are life, liberty and the pursuit of happiness."

That Declaration is reinforced by the opening words of our nation's Constitution, which declare that our union will "...establish justice, insure domestic tranquility, provide for the common defence [sic.], promote the general welfare, and secure the blessings of liberty to ourselves and our posterity..."

These two foundational statements inform our "Pledge of Allegiance," which in its poetic closing cadence declares the United States of America is "one nation, under God, with *liberty* and *justice* for all."

But what does "liberty and justice for all" mean? As an Evangelical Christian, how are my values for liberty and justice informed and shaped by my understanding of biblical liberty and biblical justice? And, finally, based on the definition of biblical liberty and justice, what is the proper role of government in the pursuit of liberty and justice for all?

LIBERTY

The Merriam-Webster dictionary defines liberty as the quality or state of being free: *a*: the power to do as one pleases *b*: freedom from physical restraint *c*: freedom from arbitrary or despotic control *d*: the positive enjoyment of various social, political, or economic rights and privileges *e*: the power of choice.

Biblically the concept of liberty (freedom) is grounded in the first chapter of the first book. Genesis 1:26-28 declares that humanity was made in the image of God, men and women in the image of God. The Hebrew word for "image" is *tselem*, which means "representative figure." The Greek form of the word is *eikon*. Caesar would send coins out throughout the Roman Empire with his *eikon* on them to declare to residents and passersby, "Caesar rules here!" We were made in the *tselem* of God; created to be God's representative figures. In verse 28 God commands humanity to multiply and fill the earth so that wherever we go, we would be a declaration that God rules here!

In the same sentence the writer of Genesis reveals what it looks like to be made in the *tselem* of God. *"...and have dominion over the fish of the sea and over the birds of the air and over every living thing that moves upon the earth."* So, the free exercise of dominion is grammatically linked to the fact that we are made in the *tselem* of God. The closest thing we have to dominion in today's language is the concept of "agency"—the ability to make choices that impact one's world. So, dominion is exercised in all of the choices one makes, large and small. Dominion requires liberty. To diminish liberty is to diminish dominion. To diminish dominion is to threaten the image of God on earth.

Thus, biblically, liberty—the freedom to exercise dominion—is intricately linked to what it means to be human—made in the image of God. Liberty is, therefore, a basic need and right of humanity.

JUSTICE

A few years ago, a friend challenged me to define "justice." "Biblically, justice is simply to make things right," I replied. He pressed further, "But how can we know what is 'right'?"

In Genesis 1:30 the writer says, at the end of the sixth day, God looked around and saw that everything in creation was "very good." The closest thing the Hebrews had to the concept of "perfection" is "very goodness," which in the Hebrew *(tov me'od)* means forcefully good. Our understanding of "perfection" was passed down to us from the Greeks. The Greek concept of perfection locates goodness or completeness within an object. The Greek word for good *(kalos)* means the object itself is without spot or blemish. The Greek word for perfect *(teleios)* means the object needs nothing more to be made complete. It is perfectly mature in itself. For the Hebrews, goodness and completeness exist in the ties between things: *tobe* is fundamentally relational. Thus, when God declares everything made in creation is *tov me'od,* God is referring to the *relationship between* all things. The relationship between humanity and God is *forcefully good.* The relationship between humanity and the rest of creation is *forcefully good*. Genesis 2 offers an intimate portrait of this relationship. Humanity named the animals, tilled the soil, and maintained the well-being of all God's creation. Likewise, the relationships between humans and their selves and between all of creation and life are both *forcefully good*. There is no shame and there is no death, disease or decay in Genesis 1 or 2. Finally, the tie between humanity and the systems that govern them are *forcefully good*. Systems are simply the way things work. So, when we look at the way things work in Genesis 1 and 2, we see that human dominion reflects God's kind of dominion. It is characterized by love, care, servanthood, reciprocity, balance, integrity, and truth.

Justice is the image of God flourishing on earth. Justice is all humanity having the liberty to exercise God's kind of dominion. Justice is right relationship between men and women, humanity and the rest of creation, all of creation and life, and humanity and the systems that govern us. Justice is present when these relationships are as they should be.

In Genesis 3 we see justice undone and it begins with a single choice. With that choice, humanity exercises a kind of dominion we haven't seen in the story so far. We see the woman and man choose to eat from the tree of the knowledge of good and evil. God had warned the humans that if they ate from the tree, they would die (Genesis 2:15- 17). The man and woman grab at their own fulfillment. They believe the serpent who tells them, "You will not die, for God knows that when you eat of it your eyes will be opened, and you will be like God, knowing good and evil." The man and woman were trying to be "like God," but they were already like God. They had been created in the *tselem* of God.

The way we think of our choices today, it barely makes sense that a choice two people make could affect all the rest of creation. That's because we think of ourselves as self-contained units, disconnected from anyone and everything else. But that is not the Hebrew worldview and it is not the world of Genesis. In this world everything is connected in a grand web of relationships. The choice of one affects all. If the peace of one is crushed, then the peace of all is pilfered. The humans are charged to exercise dominion over the rest of creation. If they exercise that dominion in the likeness of God's dominion then they will consider the needs of all before serving self. But theydon't.

As the man and woman discovered in Genesis 3, when we fail to exercise God's kind of dominion—dominion that loves and serves all—then not only do we suffer, but all relationships in creation crash and injustice finds a home. The first relationship to crash was humanity's relationship with self (Gen. 3:7), then our relationship with God (Gen 3:8-10), then between men and women (Gen. 3:11- 12,16), between humanity and the rest of creation (Gen. 3:14-15, 17-19), and then between humanity and life itself (Gen. 3:21-24). And it doesn't end there. In the next chapter brother rises up against brother (Gen. 4:8) and Cain's descendant Lamech takes two wives (Gen. 3:19) and their families are fractured. Flip a few chapters further and the relationship between lingual groups breaks at the Tower of Babel (Gen. 11:8-9) and this leads to the first break between ethnic groups. Then only three chapters later we see the first kings and with them the first wars between earthly domains.

What, then, is injustice? It is any act, structure, system, or policy that breaks any of the relationships God declared *forcefully good* in Genesis 1. Injustice is sin.

THE LIBERTY AND JUSTICE DIVIDE

The liberal/conservative polemic is a product of the modern era—an era shaped by the tyranny of "either/or" constructs. [14] But it is possible to see both truth and falsehood in a single philosophical argument. As a Christian, I believe that we live in a post-fall reality. Humanity is depraved and indeed has great capacity for evil. But I also believe that humanity has profound capacity to love. As a woman of African, Native-American, Puerto-Rican, Caribbean, Jewish, and Anglo descent, I am profoundly aware of the power of policy, systems, structures, and institutions to oppress or liberate whole people groups. I also am deeply aware of the capacity of individuals and societies to repent of their fallen inclinations toward domination, oppression, and the hoarding of resources for the benefit of self at the expense of "the other."

Biblically, Liberty and Justice lay down their arms. Humanity is given liberty in order to exercise just dominion in every sphere of life; over one's self, within the family unit, within communities, over the rest of creation, through public policy, and between nations. Just dominion is God's kind of dominion—one fundamentally characterized by love. There is no other reason for liberty in scripture. Freedom is not for the sake of "me" in scripture. It is always for the sake of "we." Liberty is given so that humanity might cultivate the *very good*-ness of all the relationships God created in the beginning and so that the *tselem* of God might flourish on earth.

The Ten Commandments serve as a model of God's kind of governance and the biblical relationship between liberty and justice.

They establish a system of governance by the rule of law, (as opposed to rule of monarchy, which the Hebrews were accustomed to after 500 years in captivity under the Pharaohs). One of the earliest known codes of law, the Ten Commandments delineate how the Israelites can re-establish *forcefully good* relationship between the people and God, each other, and with the rest of creation. The first three commands point the way to re-establish relationship with God: no other gods, no idolatry, no misuse of the name of God. The last seven commands establish the basic requirements of *forcefully good* relationship within civil society. Honoring the Sabbath institutes care for one's own soul, and protects workers, animals, and the land from exploitation. Honoring one's parents establishes good relationships within families. Then in rapid succession; no murder (respect all humanity's right to live), no adultery (protect the integrity of the family unit), no stealing (respect all humanity's right to ownership and to exercise dominion), no bearing false witness, no coveting other people's stuff (resist the temptation to become unbridled consumers of goods, people, and the rest of creation).

Through the Ten Commandments, we see God's kind of governance recognizes humanity's inclination toward evil and establishes the ethical compass by which society can discern what is good and just. The Ten Commandments also provide the basic framework of a kind of governance that levels social playing fields by protecting the inherent dignity of all without distinction of social position, class, or gender. These laws were given to a people in the midst of establishing a nation.

As much as the Ten Commandments established an ethical compass for individuals, they also served as a kind of Bill of Rights to be instituted as an early framework for how the government would interact with its people. The Israelites' governance must honor God; honor the right of all to live, must not steal from its people, and must not covet its neighboring nations' resources.

The Ten Commandments are one example of the way God re-establishes the way back to *forcefully good relationships* through just governance. Fear and notions of inherent inequality do not compel God's governance. Nor is it blind to the capacity of humanity to do evil and the need for cultivation of personal character and integrity. Rather God's governance is grounded in a fundamental belief in the capacity of humanity to exercise both degenerative acts of depravity and redemptive acts of love. God's rule of law calls individuals and society alike to walk the way of love, to cultivate the *image* of God on earth by protecting the capacity of all to exercise dominion, and to protect liberty and establish justice with equity.

Unlike the Hebrew nation, the United States of America is not a theocracy. People, not God, established our Constitution. Therefore, unlike the Ten Commandments, our Constitution is fallible, incomplete and expected to be amended as our nation matures. For example, in direct opposition to God's declaration that all humanity is equal, the Constitutional Convention of 1787 produced the Three-Fifths Compromise between the Northern and Southern states. The compromise declared enslaved people to be worth only 3/5th of a human being. Three years later, the 1790 Naturalization Act made citizenship a privilege reserved for white men only, meaning only white men were able to vote and were fully protected by the law. Enslaved black people in the south could not own land. In the context of a representative democracy, this blocked women and all people of color from exercising unfettered dominion on this land. Our nation matured and repented of its rebellion against God's truth. The 14th, 15th, and 19th Amendments to the Constitution reflect that repentance.

Also, we the people established a pluralistic democratic republic. Thus, unlike the theocratic Hebrew nation where the religious leaders were also the nation's governors, we the people are the government in the United States. We are a diverse mosaic of ethnicities, religions, genders, nationalities, histories, and values called by our founders to unite for the sake of the common good. Together, we are all ultimately responsible for the liberating or oppressive policies passed on our watch.

Liberty and justice for all can only be ensured within our systems and structures in as much as we the people abide by core fundamental values established by our founders: the value for rule of law, protection of the rights of individuals, due process, and protection of the rights of minorities. These values establish the boundaries of U.S. policy-making. They also overlap with the biblical values established in Genesis and demonstrated by the institution of the Ten Commandments. These overlapping values protect and cultivate the *image* of God on earth. They protect the ability of all to exercise dominion and they set guiding principles for how we the people will achieve a more perfect union—a *forcefully good* relationship—with one another and with the land that sustains us.

D.C. INNES

Politics is everywhere. Wherever the twos and threes are gathered, there is politics. It's in Washington, Albany, and Sacramento. It's in war and peace. It's also in commerce and compassion. It's at your workplace and in your home. You cannot ignore it, and it certainly will not ignore you. The question for anyone is not whether politics, but politics of what kind? When government is just, there is liberty. That is, when government operates within God's bounds and according to God's purposes, people are free to exercise adult self-government in godliness, and thus to enjoy the sweetness of what God meant for us in this world. But when government goes wrong, i.e., to the extent that it is unjust, it's a devouring beast.

Just government and healthy political life are intimately tied to principle. Without principle, living together politically is like trying to build a house without a plan. In the end, it will not serve you, and what you do accomplish will come down on your head. Without the right principles—that is, the principles by which God established government for our good—politics becomes simply our many attempts at self-seeking, which, as such, is not really politics at all. So it is wise for us as Christians to ask what God's design is for government and political life.

What is at stake in the breakdown of politics is easy to see in the brutal, despotic regimes that cover most of the globe. But it is more helpful for us to look closer to home.

From the 1960s into the 1990s, New York City, one of the world's great cities and America's business and cultural center, became increasingly unlivable. Though the reasons for this decline are complex, the heart of it was the failure of government to do its job and only its job. While business activity and the revenues it generated shrank, government ventured far into socially reconstructive welfare programs. But government programs require taxes, and taxes require people and businesses to pay them. The bigger the tax burden grew, however, the less incentive there was to do business in the city. To make things even worse, the programs were socially destructive, not reconstructive, encouraging welfare dependency, destroying families, and even discouraging them from forming in the first place. Still worse, the liberal establishment restrained the police whose job it was to serve the weak and vulnerable. They did this in a misguided sympathy for the criminals who were said to be victims of society. And so society rapidly disintegrated.

> The press was filled with stories of feral marauding teens, lurid killings, and brazen drive-by shootings. New Yorkers had gotten grimly used to triple-locking their doors and barring their windows and sticking NO RADIO signs in their cars, pathetically hoping to deter thieves from smashing their car windows. Some neighborhoods were like war zones, where an evening walk was fraught with danger. Police largely steered clear of these areas... Grand Central Terminal, one of the great civic spaces in America, looked like a massive, filthy homeless shelter. Parks had become open-air drug markets. City residents had to put up with constant shakedowns from aggressive beggars and "squeegee men." Ugly graffiti covered everything. The whole atmosphere of the city suggested that order had broken down.[15]

By 1994, the city had sunk so deep into civic and financial ruin that, in desperation, New Yorkers elected a Republican mayor. Rudolph Giuliani was not just another liberal New York Republican. He was a tough federal prosecutor who had successfully taken on Wall Street and the Mafia, and won the mayor's seat with a tough-on-crime platform.

As mayor, Giuliani operated on the basic principles of the Republican Party: limited government and personal responsibility. They are related. As government services expand, people's sense of personal responsibility shrinks. Myron Magnet recalls that, "Giuliani considered it no favor to a poor person to offer her a lifetime of welfare dependency, as if she were unfit for anything better. Such an approach was disrespectful, a kind of soft bigotry. Even more important, in Giuliani's view, self-respect isn't possible without self- reliance." Rather, limited government "should provide only a few key services. Its primary function, as political theorists had traditionally insisted, is ensuring that citizens are safe in the streets and in their homes."[16]

THE PURPOSE OF GOVERNMENT: PUNISH EVIL

This view of government should resonate with anyone who holds a biblically informed view of government. The Apostle Peter instructed the church,

> Be subject for the Lord's sake to every human institution, whether it be to the emperor as supreme, or to governors as sent by him to punish those who do evil and to praise those who do good. For this is the will of God, that by doing good you should put to silence the ignorance of foolish people (1 Peter 2:13-15).

The task of government is simple and limited: punish those who do evil and praise those who do good. After the flood, when God had washed all the violence from the earth, He said, "From his fellow man I will require a reckoning for the life of man. 'Whoever sheds the blood of man, by man shall his blood be shed, for God made man in his own image'" (Gen. 9:5-6). God allowed the near universal violence (Gen. 6:11) from the years between Cain and Noah to show people the crimson color of sin, that "the intention of man's heart is evil from his youth" (Gen. 8:21).

Eventually, God entrusted this coercive power of retributive justice into the hands of civil government to restrain the rapacious tendencies of sinful human beings. Without wise, tough, active government, human depravity quickly reduces the human condition to a state of pervasive and intolerable violence. When government authority breaks down—whether because of a police strike, a power outage, an invasion, or even just government indifference—outrages against property and persons follow as surely as night follows day. Without government, life would be frighteningly solitary, miserably brutish, certainly nasty and poor, and tragically short.

The Apostle Paul gives us the same teaching. The classic text for the Bible's political teaching is Romans 13, where Paul emphasizes that civil government, armed with power over life and death, "is God's servant for your good."

> Let every person be subject to the governing authorities. For there is no authority except from God, and those that exist have been instituted by God. Therefore whoever resists the authorities resists what God has appointed, and those who resist will incur judgment. For rulers are not a terror to good conduct, but to bad. Would you have no fear of the one who is in authority? Then do what is good, and you will receive his approval, for he is God's servant for your good. But if you do wrong, be afraid, for he does not bear the sword in vain. For he is the servant of God, an avenger who carries out God's wrath on the wrongdoer. Therefore one must be in subjection, not only to avoid God's wrath but also for the sake of conscience.
>
> For because of this you also pay taxes, for the authorities are ministers of God, attending to this very thing. Pay to all what is owed to them: taxes to whom taxes are owed, revenue to whom revenue is owed, respect to whom respect is owed, honor to whom honor is owed.

God appoints government for our benefit, but it is not to provide every good. It is only to prevent bad conduct with credible threat and punish it with terrible revenge[17] (v.3). Even in this, however, government's role is limited. It is beyond the scope of government to punish every failure to fulfill the debt of love. That would be to rob love of its virtuous character, and require a government with totalitarian power. The remedy would be worse than the disease.

THE PURPOSE OF GOVERNMENT: PRAISE GOOD

We see the limits of the legitimate exercise of government power in the second half of Peter's statement. Civil government is not only to punish those who do evil, but also praise those who do good. Wesley Autrey's heroic intervention on a New York subway line, and the government's response, is a clear example of this.

> Mr. Autrey was waiting for the downtown local at 137th Street and Broadway in Manhattan around 12:45 p.m. He was taking his two daughters, Syshe, 4, and Shuqui, 6, home before work. Nearby, a man collapsed, his body convulsing. The man, Cameron Hollopeter, 20, managed to get up, but then stumbled to the platform edge and fell to the tracks, between the two rails. The headlights of the No. 1 train appeared. "I had to make a split decision," Mr. Autrey said. So he made one, and leapt. Mr. Autrey lay on Mr. Hollopeter, his heart pounding, pressing him down in a space roughly a foot deep. The train's brakes screeched, but it could not stop in time. Five cars rolled overhead before the train stopped, the cars passing inches from his head, smudging his blue knit cap with grease. Mr. Autrey heard onlookers' screams. "We're O.K. down here," he yelled, "but I've got two daughters up there. Let them know their father's O.K." He heard cries of wonder, and applause.[18]

Mayor Michael Bloomberg honored Mr. Autrey at City Hall with the bronze medallion.[19] President George W. Bush praised him at the State of the Union address[20] and the United States Senate recognized him with a resolution for his "uncommon valor and tremendous bravery...by putting his own life at risk to save that of his fellow citizen." They commended him "as an example of selflessness to members of his community, his

State and the Nation."[21] Drawing official attention to good deeds of this sort has a salutary public effect. "One woman on the street told him she was glad she didn't abort her unborn child because the Subway Superman showed her that the world isn't so cruel after all."[22] Government does good when it publicizes the good among us that otherwise would go unnoticed. In so doing, it magnifies the Lord's mercy.

Government is not charged with doing the good itself. Rather, government is to encourage private citizens, communities, and citizen groups to address the many needs that arise among us, from beautification projects to helping the poor, the sick, and the homeless.

After specifying what government is to do, Peter states, "This is the will of God, that by doing good you should put to silence the ignorance of foolish people." God's will is that you, the private citizen whether on your own or with others, do good. In the Romans 13 passage, Paul points to the second table of the Law as a summary of the good that government should praise and that Christian citizens should practice. "For the commandments, 'You shall not commit adultery, You shall not murder, You shall not steal, You shall not covet,' and any other commandment, are summed up in this word: 'You shall love your neighbor as yourself'" (v.9). Civil government, when it is doing its job and only its job, provides the security in which people can serve one another in love most freely.

THE BENEFIT OF GOVERNMENT: THE DIGNITY OF LIBERTY

This is the assumption behind Paul's exhortation to Timothy. "First of all, then, I urge that supplications, prayers, intercessions, and thanksgivings be made for all people, for kings and all who are in high positions, that we may lead a peaceful and quiet life, godly and dignified in every way." (I Tim. 2:1-2) In other words, pray that your government would be good government, that it would do its job faithfully, and nothing more than that. Pray that your government, whether at the highest or lowest levels, would provide appropriate protections that allow you to "lead a peaceful and quiet life, godly and dignified in every way."

That is to say, God's purpose for civil government is that it provide an umbrella of protection for person and property that frees people to go about their business undisturbed, whether by neighbor or by government itself, providing for themselves, their neighbors, their community as whole, and anyone whom they find in need. In this way, the Bible recognizes the human dignity of liberty, that is, of taking mature account of one's own affairs.[23]

If it were government's responsibility, even in part, to do the good deeds of society, people would gradually surrender more and more private responsibility to it. For its part, government would gladly expand to take responsibility for everything it possibly could. It would soon have agencies for tying your shoes, blowing your nose, and tucking you in at night. People would become ever more narrowly selfish and childishly dependent. Advocates of activist government would justify every new good work saying, "The government has to do this because people won't do it on their own." Of course, this is precisely what has been happening over the last hundred years. Where it ends is not the sort of noble liberty that God intends for his image-bearing vice-regents. At best, you get the control of well-meaning masters over grateful slaves, or some kind of happy human zoo. At worst, and more likely, you get the totalitarian rule of a self-serving administrative class over a docile people who have entirely forgotten how to provide for themselves.[24]

Limited government is not only a good idea; it is essential to good government. Not surprisingly, it is also the biblical teaching on government. Sadly, however, it has largely eluded the human race for as long as there has been government. Many of the larger miseries of human life are traceable back to government exceeding its legitimate bounds. But government is a limited good, and so only limited government can be good. In the following chapters, I trace out the implications of this biblical principle for several issues that confront us as a nation.

CAPITALISM AND POVERTY

ON THE ROLE OF BUSINESS

ON CAPITALISM AND POVERTY

D.C. INNES

Poverty is a scandal. In the same way, death is a scandal. It's not the way the world is supposed to be, and it's an offense to the image of God in man. But the world is fallen and corrupted in sin, so there is poverty and death.

The good news, however, is that there is also redemption from sin and the consequences of sin. Christ overcame death on the cross, and He gives life to the faithful. In Him, we have hope of a new creation in which "death shall be no more, neither shall there be mourning nor crying nor pain anymore" (Rev. 21:4). There will also be super- abounding wealth. The new creation will flow with milk and honey, and the streets will be, as it were, paved with gold.

But even in this present world, the Lord mercifully provides some means of relief for our suffering. Just as we can cure diseases through understanding the way the creation works, in the same way He has given us the means to alleviate poverty. Cain plowed and reaped abundance. Joseph managed the fat years with the lean, so neither Egypt nor Israel starved. The poor will be with us always, as will sickness and death, but in our ability to understand the nature of wealth, God has given us much to relieve our distress and gladden our hearts.

God created the world a wilderness and made man from the dust of the ground. Into that earthen form He breathed life, and in the midst of the world He brought wealth from the earth and made a garden. He then placed the man in that verdant splendor, and told the man who at that point knew both the poverty of the wilderness and the wealth of the garden—to "fill the earth and subdue it and have dominion" (Gen. 1:28).

God told Adam not only to cultivate the garden, but also to extend it, making the wilderness of the world garden-like, unfolding the Lord's rich provision in an enterprise of worshipful discovery, stewardly conquest, and godly enjoyment.[25]

For example, God expected that man would tend sheep. But through animal husbandry man would develop the Shetland collie, a breed of dog well suited for shepherding. He would milk his cows, but then figure how to make yogurt and sweet clotted cream from that milk.

He would cultivate the earth to produce grains like wheat, but then go on from there to provide bread for himself, his family, his neighbors, and distant peoples who would trade with him. Not only that, he would make bagels, foccaccia, pasta, sweet pumpernickel, and fried dough. He would bring oil from the earth to light his lamps, fuel his cars, and make strong, lightweight plastics for innumerable uses in his godly endeavors.

God richly provides us with everything to enjoy (I Tim. 6:17). But it doesn't come richly to those who sit around. "Go to the ant, O sluggard; consider her ways, and be wise," the Proverbs tell us (6:6). "A little sleep, a little slumber, a little folding of the hands to rest, and poverty will come upon you like a robber, and want like an armed man" (6:10-11).

Very little wealth is just lying on the ground or growing wild, free for the taking. Prosperity comes from the intelligent, productive, and generous stewards of creation because almost all wealth is created. That is to say, it is the fruit of creative human work. For this reason, we call God's command to cultivate the-world-as-given "the creation mandate." This is partly because it was given at the creation, but also because it is a command to create. Just as God unfolded the creation in the six days following his initial ex nihilo fiat, so too He called his image-bearers to continue unfolding the wealth of the world.[26]

The natural state of this world, therefore, is not wealth, such that equitable prosperity is simply a matter of proper distribution. But nor is our natural state one of poverty, in which case justice would again be a matter of suitable distribution as it is with rations among castaways on a lifeboat.

Rather, our natural condition is one of latent wealth in poverty. Thus, overcoming the evil of poverty is not a matter of justly distributing fixed wealth, but of justly protecting people's God-given abilities to fulfill the creation mandate by creating wealth of every sort and enjoying the fruit of their labors in godliness. In that understanding, justice pertains to preserving and expanding opportunity, not redistributing booty.

Any proposed remedy for poverty is only as good as the theory of wealth that underlies it.[27] What defines the poor as poor is that they're short on wealth. There are always other problems that contribute to the poverty problem, such as political oppression or degenerate culture, but those are particular circumstances that prevent poor people from doing what they are divinely and naturally fitted to do: create wealth for themselves and their neighbors, whether it takes the form of soy beans, shoes, literature, care for one's children or parents, public administration, or pastoral leadership. The trouble with leftist Christian advocates of the poor is that, like their non-Christian counterparts, they do not understand the nature of wealth, so they cannot helpfully address the poverty problem.

Biblically, there are two ways to alleviate poverty: giving and growing.

GIVING

Psalm 41 declares, "Blessed is the one who considers the poor!" But to give, one must first have. Job was able to give generously to the poor because he was a man of means. Boaz could let Ruth glean in his field because he owned a thriving, productive estate. Joseph of Arimathea could donate a tomb for the Lord's burial because he had been making good use of his economic opportunities prior to that time.[28] Margaret Thatcher once noted that, "...even the Good Samaritan had to have the money to help, otherwise he too would have had to pass on the other side."[29]

I hasten to add that God expects not only the moneyed, but also the poor themselves, to be givers. The Apostle Paul praises the churches in Macedonia for giving generously to the relief of suffering Christians in Jerusalem despite their own "extreme poverty" (2 Cor. 8:2). It is often reported that while America is a nation of generous givers, the working classes give far more freely than the wealthy.[30]

Simple almsgiving can be problematic, however. In the prosperous West, we are largely confused about who is poor and who is not. The biblical poor are those in terrible need. They are essentially helpless, often the widow, the orphan, and the sojourner—people without defenders and without the means to defend themselves and to provide for their most basic needs. When Job speaks of defending the poor, he mentions the widow, the fatherless, and those in danger of perishing from hunger and exposure. (Job 31:16-23) They are exposed to the wolves of society, powerful and unscrupulous people of means who would devour them for selfish gain. They are not people on the verge of canceling their cable TV.[31] Paul counseled deacons to help only the genuine poor. "Honor widows who are truly widows" (I Tim. 5:3-14).

It is worth noting that in his remarks on caring for helpless widows, Paul makes no mention of the civil government. He issues no call for Christians to protest the "injustice" of the Roman government leaving the poor without food and work.

In giving to the destitute, givers should also make sure that their compassion is effective, and not a mere sop to the conscience that does unintentional harm. Indiscriminate giving to panhandlers encourages shameless fakes to take to the streets in great numbers for free money. As people become more generous in their handouts, one can expect begging to become more organized and exploitative.

In the film *Slumdog Millionaire*, a man burns the eyes of an orphan to make the boy's begging more lucrative. This happens in countries where almsgiving is common. In Albania, I saw a young gypsy man with no arms or legs set out shirtless in a busy square. Is it possible that he had been run over by train, and survived with only his torso? From what I was told, it is all too likely that someone maimed him as a child, perhaps a stepfather or captor, so that he would elicit greater sympathy and attract more generous giving. Charity must be wise.

GROWING

While giving to the poor is an explicit command, the other means of providing for them, such as growing a business or growing the economy in general, are implied but nonetheless real. The Bible does not show us simply "haves" and "have-nots," with the kind-hearted haves doling out alms to the have-nots. Like life itself, the picture is more complex.

Employers and employees prosper together (John 4:36; I Cor. 9:9- 10), though the latter depend on the initiative of the former. After the famine passed, Boaz saw a great harvest, paid many people to help him reap, and left plenty behind for gleaners like Ruth. Even wicked Nabal, Abigail's appalling husband who was "very rich," shared his bounty with his shepherds and shearers (I Sam. 25).

Because employers are in a position to bless simply by virtue of being employers, God gives them moral instruction. They are to pay their workers on time (Deut. 24:15). They are also to pay a customary wage: "The laborer deserves his wages" (Luke 10:7). But it is not the employer's responsibility to fund all his employees into the middle class, regardless of their work. Job paid his servants generously, but he was limited by market constraints. They remained servants.

I once knew a fellow who claimed that he loved his neighbor when he bought stock in IBM. If that were the limit of his charitable efforts, he would not be living a recognizably Christian life. Nonetheless, he had a point. Not everyone who invests is acting in love, but you can wisely invest your money with your neighbor's good in mind. It is said that Ronald Reagan often gave to people in need, quietly writing a check to someone who wrote to him with a sad personal story. But he did far more for the poor by slashing marginal tax rates and freeing people to generate the longest period of economic growth in the twentieth century.

THE MARKET, THE POOR, AND THE TWO PARTIES

As a young man working summer jobs, I learned an important lesson: always use the right tool for the job. At a day job in a warehouse, I needed to cut the plastic straps surrounding a sealed box so I could unpack a washing machine. I looked for something sharp, and found a screwdriver. That's sharp! So I began stabbing at the straps with the screwdriver. (I can see you wincing. I'm wincing too. Ah, youth!) Of course, I missed the straps, pierced the cardboard, and dented the appliance. Lesson learned: never use a tool for any purpose it was not designed to serve. If you do, you are sure to break something or hurt someone.

Government is a tool of God's design, and He gave it for a purpose: punishing evil and praising good. When we try to use it to do the good that it should only praise in others, wealth is destroyed and people are demoralized. We see the truth of that proposition working itself out in Europe where they have chosen the path of socialism, or social democracy, for the last sixty years. Now many of those countries find themselves with national debts the size of their annual gross domestic products, the total value of all the goods and services they produce in a year. There is a word for that: bankruptcy. (Basket case would be a less technical term.)

In America, Democrats, in their efforts to help people, are taking us down that European road of state provision. Government schools.

School-provided lunches. School-provided breakfasts. School-provided abortions. Government financed student loans. Government control of all colleges and universities making use of student loans. Government home financing. Government engineered housing bubble. Government rescue from the resulting financial crisis. Government environmental protection, workplace safety standards, and multiple layers of bureaucratic intrusion that drive your employer out of business. Government unemployment insurance. Government old age pension. Government medical care for the elderly. Government medical care for the poor. Government medical care for everybody. The I.R.S. to make sure that ten percent of the country is paying for all of this.

But though we may bankrupt ourselves paying for these programs and for an ever-expanding class of free riders whom the political class is happy to take on as clients, surely we at least have the moral satisfaction of knowing that we are a compassionate society. But no, we lose that too.

Government charity (a contradiction in terms) wicks the charity out of the people themselves. As government assumes increasingly more responsibility for charitable work, private citizens come to feel increasingly less inclination, and recognize increasingly less responsibility, for it. Advocates of government charity then point to this private inactivity as justification for evermore expanded activity in this field.

Again, look at Europe. They have a generous welfare state that provides a far wider array of social services than ours does in America. In the Netherlands, the government provides parents with a stipend to feed and clothe their children. Why should parents feed and clothe their own children? And what about the aged? No problem. If your mother has arthritis, the government will send someone over to fix her faucets and change all the handles on her doors. Why should her children bother themselves with such things?

A friend of mine who left the Netherlands twenty years ago but who still has family there, including his aged mother, tells me that, precisely because of the generosity and even the efficiency of government provision, people have become personally unmindful of the needy. Even within families, personal relations are colder, he says, more businesslike. The Dutch have decided that a good society is a compassionate society, and so people should provide for one another's dignity and basic quality of life—but only through the state. People needn't actually have anything to do with one another directly.

The American political left is eagerly working to make our country more like Europe.[32] They see our individualism as selfish and immoral, and they view reliance on private charity as ineffective and degrading in comparison to government services and entitlements. The lesson of the Dutch experience, however, is not that the welfare state is the defining feature of a compassionate society, but that our choice in providing for the helpless and suffering is between the nanny state and a caring citizenry.[33]

The Christian moral objection to the welfare state is not only that it corrupts the character of those who otherwise would have responsibility for giving, but also that it violates the eighth commandment. One of government's fundamental tasks is to protect people in their property. "Thou shalt not steal." God instituted government in part to protect people against being despoiled by their neighbors. Man being sinful, there will always be some who would rather take the fruit of someone else's labor than labor on their own. Theft, in that regard, is a kind of slavery. It forces the victim against his will to work for the thief.

Thieves come in different forms. They can be particular people or they can gather in a mob, in which case we call their theft "pillage." Mobs can be crude, such as when they rampage, or they can be sophisticated. A sophisticated mob, when it wants to pillage a propertied minority, knows that rather than fight the government, it can use the government. After all, the government's power to secure property is also the power to take it away. When a mob uses government to pillage its more propertied neighbors, we call it progressive taxation, or redistribution of wealth. Sometimes we call it fairness. But it is theft all the same.

I wish I could say that the Republican Party embraces all these principles fully, consistently, and with deep conviction and understanding. Alas, that is too much to expect in a fallen world. None of us is perfectly true to the principles we profess. Why should we expect greater fidelity from a political party?

Human frailty always creates a gap between ideals and institutions, between principles and practice.[34] A party, like the country as a whole, is sometimes closer and sometimes farther from its ideals. But small government and a free economy for the liberty, prosperity, and ultimately happiness of the people are the principles the Republican Party upholds. Despite the shortcomings and departures of the two Bush administrations, despite McCain-Feingold,[35] No Child Left Behind,[36] prescription drug entitlements,[37] and a binge of government pork-barrel spending under Republican watch, the GOP is still in principle the party of Reagan. For that reason, a faithful political warrior can call the party back to these principles. But whereas in the Republican Party someone appealing to these principles is a reformer, among Democrats, he's a revolutionary.

LISA SHARON HARPER

Business is not the devil and neither is money. Business is just people providing goods or services for money, and money is just paper—or metal. In and of themselves, money and business have neither positive nor negative value. They just are. There are plenty of business people mentioned in scripture. Consider the Proverbs 31 woman. An entrepreneur, "She makes linen garments and sells them; she supplies the merchants with sashes." Consider Lydia of Thyatira, a dealer in purple cloth, who the writer of Acts lists by name (Acts 16:14). Consider four of the twelve disciples: Peter, Andrew, James, and John who were likely owners of a fishing cooperative in Galilee.[38] Consider the parable where Jesus compares the Kingdom of Heaven to a merchant who sells everything to buy one pearl. Jesus used the language of profit to help his hearers understand the immense value of the Kingdom of God.

Business and money are important and socially valuable, but they bring up two important questions: 1) How does human depravity fuel our chosen economic system—the system of expansionary free- market capitalism? and 2) How do the outcomes of that system square with God and God's purposes on earth? To begin to answer these questions, we will start with God and the latter question and work our way to the first.

Luke opens the book of Acts by immediately setting the political scene: "In the days of King Herod of Judea". The eldest son of Herod the Great, King Herod of Judea (also known as Archelaus) took after his father. He was a repressive leader who carried on his father's love for massive building projects that exploited Israel's large lower class. Herod used his people to build structures that reinforced the power and status of the occupying empire. Archelaus ruled until 6 AD when Judea became a Roman province. Judea, at that time, is under repressive rule and people are being exploited for the sake of the expansion of empire. It is into this context Jesus is born.

Approximately thirty years later, Herod Antipas is the prefect of Rome when Jesus stands in his hometown synagogue. He is handed the scroll. He unrolls it, finds Isaiah 61 and reads:

> *The Spirit of the Lord is upon me,*
> *Because He has anointed me*
> *To bring good news to the poor.*
> *He has sent me to proclaim release to the captives*
> *And recovery of sight to the blind, to let the oppressed go free,*
> *To proclaim the year of the Lord's favor.*

Jesus rolls up the scroll, sits down and says, "Today this scripture has been fulfilled in your hearing." In other words, *you know how Isaiah said one day someone would proclaim these things. Well, I just did! It's on. The year of the Lord's favor is on*!

OBSERVING THE SABBATH

The Year of Jubilee (Leviticus 25:8-55) was the centerpiece of an economic system instituted by God as the Israelites entered the Promised Land. In this system every seven years the Israelites were commanded to observe the Sabbatical year (Leviticus 25:1-7, Deuteronomy 15:1-18). During this year, all debts were forgiven, slaves were set free and the land was given rest from all sowing and reaping. In this theocratic agrarian society, Sabbatical year was a major regulatory act that imposed a yearlong cycle of rest for workers and the land in addition to the weekly Sabbath, which God instituted through the Ten Commandments. The Sabbatical year also affected merchants' bottom lines. Labor is a critical cost of production. That cost is a key factor in the ability of business to make a profit. Thus, we must understand, the command to free their slaves every seven years would have a profound effect on the ability of businesses to expand profits to the point of empire.

The Year of Jubilee came at the end of seven seven-year cycles. In the fiftieth year, not only would debts be forgiven, slaves freed, and the land given rest, but also all land was returned to its original deed- holders, effectively banning outright sale of land and only allowing land to be leased for fifty years or less.

This government regulation reinforced the view among the Israelites that natural resources belong to God, not humanity. We are simply the stewards of land entrusted to us temporarily by God.

It also created conditions that would prevent any Israelite household from falling into multi-generational poverty. After 49 years, even the most destitute would reclaim the land given to their ancestors as they entered the Promised Land. The Year of Jubilee functioned as an equalizing reset button among the Israelites, preventing the accumulation of gross wealth and the entrenchment of gross poverty.

While the United States is not a theocracy, Israel's Year of Jubilee offers a useful picture of the priorities within God's economy. In God's economy, unlimited business growth is not an expectation. Rather, God imposes regulations on the business sector that prevent their growth from reaching the point of empire. In God's economy, the well-being of workers and the land matters. God's regulations limit exploitation and offer conditions conducive to flourishing by providing Sabbath and Sabbatical-year rest for workers and the land and by offering Jubilee debt forgiveness for all those enslaved to pay off debt. In God's economy, there is no interest on loans to fellow Israelites. (Deuteronomy 23:19) In God's economy, private individual ownership of land does not exist. Rather, land is owned by God alone and exists for the common good of all the people and of the wild animals that live on the land. (Leviticus 25:1-7)

This is what God's dominion looks like. It is this dominion that Jesus announced as He read the Isaiah 61 prophecy in that Nazarene synagogue. The Year of Jubilee and the reign of God were at hand, and they stood in direct opposition to the kind of dominion practiced by King Herod and the Roman Empire. With his Luke 4 pronouncement, Jesus declares a divine revolt against the unjust systems and seditious priorities of the kingdoms of men. In Jesus' proclamation we see that the dominion of God prioritizes the disenfranchised, the marginalized, the oppressed, and the poor. And we see, above all else, that Jesus has come so that the image of God might flourish in people, not the image of earthly kings on coins.

ECONOMIC NEO-LIBERALISM GAINS ROOTS

From 1980 until the 2008 global market crash, the chosen economic system of the United States was a neo-liberal brand of free-market capitalism. The three pillars of basic capitalism are private ownership, profit motive, and the cultivation of a competitive market. True free-market capitalism is distinguished by its total trust in market supply and demand to maintain economic balance in society with limited government intervention. Economic neo-liberalism, not to be confused with political liberalism, is an economic concept with roots in the modern Conservative movement.[39] The concept gained a foothold in U.S. economic policy during Ronald Reagan's two terms in the oval office. The goal of neo-liberalism is to transfer control of the economy from the public to private sector. Neo-liberals (also referred to as free-market fundamentalists) believe that this transfer will make government more efficient and the economy more nimble and able to respond to market demands.

Neo-liberal economic policies were most notably enshrined in the 1989 Washington Consensus, a consensus of the World Bank, the International Monetary Fund (IMF), and the U.S. Department of Treasury. The national and international outcomes of the Consensus and our chosen economic system include: 1) radical deregulation of international corporations and the banking industry, 2) privatization of public resources and utilities, 3) consent for offshore tax shelters and deep tax-cuts for the top tier of tax payers and increased taxes for the middle class and the poor through wage and consumption taxes, 4) the demise of unions, and 5) the pact between the World Bank, IMF, and the U.S. Treasury forced every developed and developing economy in the world to allow the market to govern everything.[40] Thus most of the world lived under the market's dominion.

WORKERS AND THE POOR CARRY THE BURDEN

This chosen economic system laid the bulk of burden on the shoulders of workers and the poor. When Reagan won the 1980 presidential election the average household debt was approximately 48 percent of the nation's Gross Domestic Product (GDP). By December 2009, household debt had ballooned to 96 percent of GDP.[41] Mortgage foreclosure rates were 0.31 percent in 1980[42] and 14.4 percent by late 2009.[43] Likewise, in

1981, the unemployment rate was 7.1 percent compared to just past 20 percent by November 2009.

The international effects have been even more devastating. The neo- liberal agenda and the Washington Consensus initiated deep deregulation of multi-national corporations, multiple ways to avoid paying taxes to the nations upon whose land the corporations did business, and private monopolization of public utilities.

The deregulation of multi-national corporations made it possible for them to exploit land and workers, catalyzing greater deforestation, which contributed to an accelerated rate of global warming and displaced indigenous peoples from tribal lands and resources.[44] To boot, the Washington Consensus expressly enabled corporations to utilize offshore tax shelters to maximize corporate profits.

If neo-liberal free-market capitalism left a wide wake of devastation, it also left a yawning gap between its victims and its benefactors. Who actually benefitted from tax-cuts and offshore tax shelters, deregulation, and privatization? When Reagan took office, the marginal tax rate for top-tier earners was 70 percent. Today, the nation's top tax tier only contributes 35 percent of its income to the nation's common purse.[45] Reagan pledged to kill unions and slash taxes for top tier earners upon entering office in 1981. In 1980, nearly 20 percent of private sector jobs in the U.S. were unionized. At that time the average CEO salary was approximately $1 million. By 2007, fewer than 7 percent of American workers were unionized and the average CEO salary had multiplied eleven times to nearly $11 million.[46] In 1980 the ratio of CEO to worker wages was 42 to 1.[47] By 2008, the ratio of S&P500 firm CEOs' pay to average U.S. workers' pay was 319 to 1. The ratio of CEO to minimum wage worker pay was 740 to 1 in the same year.[48]

CAN CAPITALISM BE REDEEMED?

Recently, I sat at a conference table with 10 students at Waynesburg University, a Christian college located in the heart of southwest Pennsylvania's coal country, south of Pittsburgh. I had spoken on the concept of *shalom* (biblical peace) in the morning chapel service, so one student wanted to know what I thought of capitalism in light of God's goal to reconcile all relationships declared *very good* in Genesis 1, which includes the relationship between humanity and the systems that govern us. Kyle, a sharp senior, asked: "Can capitalism be redeemed?"

I replied, "I'd rather not talk about capitalism generally. I'd rather talk about our actual economic system. So, if you ask can neo-liberal, free-market capitalism be redeemed, the answer is, "I don't think so." The premises upon which it stands are inherently in direct opposition to the purposes of God. I shared a quote from Jerome Guillet, an investment banker in the energy sector in France. He was interviewed in the documentary "The End of Poverty?" Guillet said flatly: "Famines are effective market solutions. They reduce demand. If we leave it to the markets, that's what we have. If there's not enough food, then some people will die and that reduces demand and the market is balanced. It's an effective market solution."[49] In that system, the market takes the place of God. The market rules and, as an accepted consequence, millions of images of God are crushed. Now, if you ask me, do you think neo-liberal, free-market capitalism can be dismantled and replaced with a more just system? The answer is, "Absolutely. We chose free-market capitalism. We can un-choose it. Human actors constructed our economic system; human actors can deconstruct it."

Aneel Karnani, an associate professor of strategy at the University of Michigan's Stephen M. Ross School of Business, warns in a Wall Street Journal (WSJ) article:[50] "The fact is that while companies sometimes can do well by doing good, more often they can't. Because in most cases, doing what's best for society means sacrificing profits." He explains further, "Executives are hired to maximize profits; that is their responsibility to their company's shareholders. Even if executives wanted to forgo some profit to benefit society, they could expect to lose their jobs if they tried—and be replaced by managers who would restore profit as the top priority."

THE REGULATION OF GOVERNMENT

"The ultimate solution," Karnani says, "is government regulation. Its greatest appeal is that it is binding. Government has the power to enforce regulation. No need to rely on anyone's best intentions." In a WSJ podcast interview Karnani uses the problem of pollution as an example:[51]

> Karnani: When companies manufacture certain products, they pollute the environment. The only way to produce less pollution is for the company to make less profit. We cannot expect companies to do this voluntarily out of some sense of corporate responsibility motive. So, now we need society to set pollution standards. That is the role of government. That is the role of the political mechanisms we have set up in society to determine the appropriate pollution levels that we are willing to tolerate.
>
> Interviewer: Does that regulation also impact shareholders of the company?
>
> Karnani: Absolutely. When we regulate pollution like that it will penalize the company, because it will have to follow these standards. So, for example, companies are not allowed to burn sulfur coal and they are mandated to put in place some pollution- reducing equipment. This clearly hurts profits, but we think it's in society's interests to do this.
>
> Interviewer: So, maybe the shareholders are less upset about taking those necessary steps?

> Karnani: They might be upset, but they have to follow the law. And it's up to society to make these trade-offs between profits and, in this particular case, pollution.

Author and historian Clifford Cobb, makes several practical recommendations for the dismantling of global neo-liberal, free-market capitalism. In addition to government regulation of multi-national corporations, Cobb recommends debt forgiveness for undeveloped and developing countries, the end of privatization of natural resources, and land reform such that the people who work the land own it—not multi-national corporations. In ancient Israel, God constructed a system where the Israelites could only lease land, because the land was for the good of the nation not individuals and ultimately it belonged to God. Likewise, land reform might only allow corporations to lease land under regulatory standards set by the developing country and with the understanding that the people own the land.[52]

Cobb also recommends restructuring taxes by doing away with wage and consumption taxes, which make the bulk of the burden fall on workers and the poor. Rather, Cobb says, "If justice is to be done, most of the taxes should fall on property ownership and not on wages, not on people."

In God's economy and in today's world, justice for all humanity requires appropriate limitation of liberty for businesses. It requires that we bow to the will of God concerning the well-being of people made in God's image. It requires that we value people more than money. It requires that we repent from our addiction to growth and consumption. Businesses don't have to be empires. It is usually best for society when they are not. Above all, we must depose the dominion of the market. The market is not God. God is God.

PART 3

CONVERSATIONS

MY BROTHER'S KEEPER

ON HEALTH CARE

ON HEALTH CARE

LISA SHARON HARPER

I have a friend who survived cancer—twice. His patience was stretched to the brink recently when he found himself in a heated debate with a stranger he met at a business event. The stranger quipped, "Government should have nothing to do with health care." My friend, Andrew, an educated, accomplished man who worked as a chemical engineer and then as a marketer for a top pharmaceutical company and earned his MBA from a world-class business school, tried to appeal to the stranger's conscience asking, "What about the working class woman with no insurance who gets cancer, but doesn't know until it's too late because she can't get regular check-ups because she has no insurance?" The stranger replied, "She can go to the emergency room." Andrew was shocked. By the time this hypothetical woman is in enough pain that she is forced to go to the emergency room, it will be too late. Plus, there's this: "Since when," he asked, "does the emergency room offer radiation or chemotherapy?"

Andrew's hypothetical woman with no insurance has a name—18,163,716 names in the U.S. to be exact.[53] One such name caught my attention, but she didn't have cancer. She had lupus.

Monique "Nikki" White was a college graduate who worked in a hospital trauma ward and wanted to be a doctor. She grew up in the Appalachian Mountains of northeastern Tennessee where she was an honor student, took ballet lessons, and played soccer and basketball. At age 13, Nikki started having such severe pain in her stomach that it forced her to stop playing basketball. By 21, she was diagnosed with lupus, a disease in which the immune system attacks healthy tissue. Lupus has no cure, but most people who have it live normal life spans through a rigorous regimen of specialists and medications.

In 2001, Nikki's lupus worsened. She had to quit her job in a hospital trauma unit and move into a garage apartment on her parents' property. She lost her insurance. Eventually, she enrolled in her state's Medicaid system, TennCare, but was dropped from that in 2005 due to state budget cuts.[54]

When lesions spread to her hands she wore gloves to take copious notes about her condition. She wrote in journals, on napkins, and on pieces of paper that marked her place in her Bible. One note read: "Awake choking on blood running down back of throat; nose bleed ensued shortly afterward. Good amount of blood covering my face, teeth, in my mouth. Lasted about 10 minutes...Surging pains in my head, but deeper, as if in my brain. Pulsing pain continued intermittently. Really frightened, tried not to panic."[55]

On her 32nd birthday, in early November 2005, Nikki had such severe pain she couldn't open her presents. "Three weeks later, as lesions spread over her body and her stomach swelled, she couldn't sleep."[56]

"Mama, please help me! Please take me to the E.R.," she howled, according to her mother, Gail Deal. "OK, let's go," Mrs. Deal recalls saying.

"No, I can't," the daughter replied. "I don't have insurance."[57]

Nikki had a stroke the next morning and was rushed to the emergency room anyway. The hospital performed several surgeries to repair the damaged organs and Nikki stayed in the hospital at its expense for months, but it was too late. Six months later Nikki was dead.[58]

Eight days later Nikki's parents received a form letter addressed to Nikki, informing her she had been approved to receive Tennessee's Medicaid. "You don't have to wait until you get your TennCare card to get care or medicine," the letter said. "Just take this letter with you."[59]

U.S. HEALTH CARE PLAYS FAVORITES

Nikki was created in the image of God. As such, her life warrants all the respect, care, and protection afforded to one created in the image of God. The fact that she bore God's image endowed Nikki with the intrinsic right to live—a right protected by the Constitution of the United States and by the Universal Declaration of Human Rights.[60] But health care in the U.S. plays favorites with lives, offering some more access to care and protection of their lives than others.

Forty-two percent of U.S. adults are underinsured or uninsured, according to a 2008 study conducted by the Commonwealth Fund. The word *underinsured* describes people whose current high insurance deductible, lifetime caps, or limited coverage would present the individual or family with serious economic hardship in the case of any serious health needs.[61] The study found that in 2007 uninsured and underinsured adults were more likely to have low or moderate incomes.

> About seven in ten underinsured adults had annual incomes below $40,000 or below 300 percent of poverty—similar to the income distribution of the uninsured. In contrast, nearly two-thirds of those with more adequate insurance had incomes above $40,000. Underinsured adults were more likely than either of the other two groups to have health problems.[62]

In other words, in the U.S., the right to live is earned through economic fortune or white-collar work. Life is not, in practice, an intrinsic right; the right to live is bought—at a high price.

For nearly 100 years, U.S. presidents have tried to move the reality of our health care system into alignment with our nation's declared values for life, freedom and equal protection under the law. They aspired to transform a system that disproportionately claims the lives of middle and low-income people into one that actively protects the lives of all. Yet, at every turn, they have been met with opposition from an equally strong value-driven American tradition—Laissez-faire conservatism, which helped make the United States a nation of entrepreneurs. [63]

Theodore Roosevelt advocated for a national health insurance program in 1912, and in 1935 President Franklin D. Roosevelt tried to include a national health insurance program in Social Security. But the American Medical Association (AMA) was among the first to cry foul during FDR's bid. They feared the new system would cut into doctors' newly lucrative profits, thus threatening the prosperity of American entrepreneurs.

On November 19, 1945 President Harry S. Truman sent a letter to Congress proposing the nation's first "single payer" program—an optional national health care fund that recipients would pay into monthly to receive medical benefits.[64] The AMA eviscerated him. They leveled the charge for the first time that universal health care is "socialized medicine." This was especially significant as the charge came on the brink of the Cold War. Ironically, no Communist country had a system anything like Truman's proposal. On the contrary, even then, America held the unique distinction of being the only industrial nation in the free world without national health insurance.

The idea of Medicare was a central platform of John F. Kennedy's 1960 presidential campaign. He thought it unconscionable to maintain a system where seniors, who were usually poor because they could not work, also lacked health care because of the historic ties between the provision of healthcare and work in the United States. Kennedy's fight for Medicare launched immediately after his inauguration in January 1961, but failed to push past the cries of the AMA and private insurers who accused Kennedy of promoting socialized medicine. [65]

Medicare didn't resurface until 1965 when President Lyndon B. Johnson proposed an amendment to FDR's Social Security Act to include Medicare. The AMA, insurers, and the Republican Party pulled out all the stops. This time, they enlisted the help of Hollywood actor and rising conservative activist, Ronald Reagan, who recorded an album predicting that Medicare would trigger the rise of socialized medicine and the end of American freedom and values. The bill still passed and overnight 19 million senior citizens gained access to health care.

In 1974 Republican president Richard Nixon proposed the Comprehensive Health Insurance Act, which would have offered state and federal subsidies to expand the wildly popular Medicare and Medicaid programs to cover all Americans not currently covered by the workplace. The Nixon plan was the closest the U.S. ever came to attaining universal health care, but congress missed its chance when political wrangling from the left stalled the process long enough for Nixon to announce his resignation in light of Watergate.[66] AMA, private insurers, and Republicans were notably silent.

In 1993 President Bill Clinton assembled a Health Reform Task Force that conceived a bill that would retain the best of the private market, while offering universal coverage, total health security, system integration, and cost containment. But the hydra reared its heads again with the same charge—"socialized medicine"—exacerbating a combination of factors, including: bad political timing, bad process, and acute voter anxiety.[67]

THE PATIENT PROTECTION AND AFFORDABLE CARE ACT IS PASSED

Then, 97 years after Theodore Roosevelt first proposed a national healthcare system, President Barack Obama mounted one of the most dramatic struggles ever witnessed within the halls of Congress. Often compared to a roller-coaster ride, maybe it was. Congress endured a long, windy, loop-de-loop, stomach churning process throughout 2009 and into early

2010. Then came the Obama administration's lightening-speed quest for passage of The Patient Protection and Affordable Care Act.

After a long and windy tactical fight that excluded any single-payer bill as an option from the start, the administration enlisted five congressional subcommittees to present bill options and brought the AMA to the table. This key historic nemesis of health reform endorsed the Obama healthcare plan in July '09. But the victory was short lived. The administration suffered setbacks of misinformation and public hysteria at town hall meetings throughout the August '09 recess.

National debate zeroed in on the "public option," which was designed to rival private market options, thus bringing overall costs down and offering middle and low income Americans true choice. The House narrowly passed its version of the bill in late 2009 with a public option included and the Senate passed its version by an even narrower margin on Christmas Eve 2009 with no public option.

Just as the House and Senate were working to merge their bills and everyone thought they could exhale, the Massachusetts special election of January 2010 threw a curveball across the Senate floor. Scott Brown, a Republican who campaigned that he would become the final necessary vote to filibuster the merged bill in the Senate, was elected to replace deceased Senator Ted Kennedy. Overnight, the Democrats lost their 60-seat supermajority. They were no longer filibuster-proof.

In February, President Obama brought Republicans and Democrats together for a seven-hour televised Health Care Summit. Each side made its case. Democrats explained that the final provisions of the bill are actually centrist and would honor the wishes of mainstream voters. Republicans said the bill was out of touch with mainstream America and that the bill should be thrown out and begun again from scratch.

In the end, President Obama, House Speaker Nancy Pelosi and Senate Majority Leader Harry Reid agreed to take the Senate version of the bill back to the House and pass that version through a budget reconciliation process, which prohibits use of the filibuster. On March 21, the House approved the Senate version of the bill. Later that week the House and Senate approved minor "fixes" and President Obama signed the bill into law on Tuesday, March 23, 2010.[68]

The Patient Protection and Affordable Care Act will protect the sanctity of the lives for a record 30 million more Americans. It will add 16 million people to the Medicaid rolls and will subsidize private coverage for low and middle-income people like Nikki White. It will regulate insurance companies more closely, preventing them from denying coverage to Americans with pre-existing conditions and outlawing lifetime caps on coverage. It will cost the federal government $938 billion over the next ten years, according to the non-partisan Congressional Budget Office. But when all is said and done, the law will cut enough costs that it will actually reduce the federal deficit by $138 billion in the same period and by more than $1 trillion over the second decade.[69]

In his victory speech President Obama offered perspective: "Today, after almost a century of trying; today after more than a year of debate; today after all the votes have been tallied, health insurance reform becomes law in the United States of America."[70]

Jesus said, "No slave can serve two masters; for a slave will either hate the one and love the other, or be devoted to the one and despise the other. You cannot serve God and wealth." (Matthew 6:24) No tug of war in American politics illustrates this scripture more than the epic battle for health reform in the United States. America's deep value for equal protection of the lives of people created in the image of God has been pitted against the deeply-held value of rugged individualism and the entrepreneurial spirit. Both are important. Both make America what it has become. But in a representative democracy our private values affect millions of human lives. So, when push comes to shove, followers of Jesus must open our eyes and see the effects of our ideological loyalties on real people made in Gods' image—people like Nikki.

Jesus reminds us that our creator requires supreme loyalty. If we claim to follow Jesus, then we are to be slaves to the God who "made heaven and earth, the sea, and all that is in them; who keeps faith forever; who executes justice for the oppressed; who gives food to the hungry" (Psalm 146:6-7). If we claim to be followers of Jesus, then we must be slaves to the God who protects and cultivates the lives of people made in his image as He "opens the eyes of the blind" and "lifts up those who are bowed down" (Psalm 146:8)—slaves not only in our individual morality, but also in our vote. Wealth, Jesus warns, will make you hate God. It will demand your supreme loyalty. It will call you to conspire in the crushing of the image of God on earth. It will demand the sacrifice of human lives on its altar. "You cannot serve God and wealth," Jesus said.

So I ask: As the Health Reform law is enacted over the next decade; as states file lawsuits to overturn the law; as the courts take up the constitutionality of the law, how should Jesus followers respond? There are still approximately 12 million uninsured or underinsured lives that remain unprotected under the current health reform law. We must call for more. We must call for universal care that protects and cultivates the image of God in all of us.

D.C. INNES

The Bible is a book for Sunday through Saturday. It addresses all of life because the lordship of Christ reaches to every corner of creation. "Take captive every thought," wrote the Apostle Paul, "to obey Christ" (2 Cor. 10:5). With this in mind, Dutch theologian Abraham Kuyper claimed, "There is not a square inch in the whole domain of our human existence over which Christ, who is Sovereign over all, does not cry: 'Mine!'"[71]

The American health care system must be no exception to that principle. What, then, is the biblically Christian position on health care reform? Does love command universal, government-run health care? I don't see how that's possible, because God has not given the responsibility for the delivery and financing of medical services to the civil government. Does God care about our health? Yes, but not through the civil government. Medical services are one of the many goods that people provide for themselves and for one another in a properly functioning economy. Insofar as providing these goods for the helpless is concerned, it is a good deed that government praises but does not itself undertake.

So biblically, health care is none of the government's business, aside from regulating it to the extent that public safety requires. Your health care, and the care of your neighbor in need, is your business. So if there is a Christian approach to addressing our current health care questions, it proceeds from a biblical understanding of human nature, personal responsibility, commerce, and caring for the poor.

OUR CURRENT PROBLEM IS AN INSURANCE PROBLEM

After eating a packaged cookie containing Brazil nuts, my son's face and throat swelled up like a party balloon. Since it was 8 o'clock at night, we headed for the emergency room. We have health insurance, but to reduce our monthly fees we carry a large deductible, and so a few weeks later we received bills for over $1,000. That's a lot of money for sitting all night in an examining room waiting for a doctor to look at my son and prescribe some medicine.

The reason for the ridiculously high price tag and the just as ridiculously slow service is that our health care system is not consumer-based, but insurance-company based. As it gets progressively government-based, the system will become even worse.

John Stossel states our problem nicely: "America's health care problem is not that some people lack insurance—it's that 250 million Americans do have it."[72]

You buy insurance to protect yourself against the unlikely but real possibility of ruinous disaster. It would ruin you financially if your house were to burn down or if you were to require extensive treatment for a serious and debilitating illness. Because everyone faces and fears the same unlikely possibility, people voluntarily group together to pay a small amount into a large pool, agreeing to compensate any contributor who finds himself in one of these unhappy circumstances.

Insurance is a prudent way of managing risk communally.

But risk and rarity are essential to the insurance concept. Your home insurance does not cover leaky faucets, lawn care, or even replacing your roof, as costly as that is. These are common and predictable expenses. So, too, your car insurance does not cover gas, oil changes, and scheduled maintenance visits. You don't buy insurance for clothing and groceries.

Even though these are necessities, it is neither your employer's nor the government's responsibility to provide you with insurance to cover them. You pay for them out of your regular income. It's why you have income. If you have difficulty paying for any of these things, you budget more wisely, generate more income, or, in exceptional cases, turn to the kindness of family, deacons, or private charity. "Go to the ant, O sluggard" (Prov. 6:6-11)

So why do we treat medical insurance differently? We demand that it cover everything from cancer treatment to check-ups. And people get angry if their employer-provided health insurance doesn't cover every minor benefit. Your coverage is "lousy." But what ought to be minor expenses have become costly precisely because everyone is paying for them through insurance instead directly out of their own pockets.[73]

Getting insurance out of the little things is nowhere in view. We have had this nonsensical health insurance regime since World War II, and it seems we're stuck with it. So how do we make the most of it? Do we infuse it with more government decision-making, or with more consumer decision-making?

LOWERING COSTS

In 2009, Americans were projected to spend 17.6 percent of their GDP on health care, proportionately far higher than any other country.[74] And that was two years before the first baby boomer retired! Lowering the cost of services requires increasing the responsiveness of service providers to consumers. As in any other industry, the market does the work. If employers were to give the money they now spend on health insurance directly to employees as tax- sheltered cash income, people could then buy whatever package they think is right for them. Insurance companies and health care providers would start tailoring their services to consumer needs instead of to the employer's HMO. Re-establishing the link between the consumer and cost concerns would bring down prices as doctors, hospitals, and companies began competing for business from stingy yet quality-conscious consumers. It works everywhere else in the economy.

The opposite approach is a state-run health care system, the Democratic dream.[75] Advocates sell it to the public as the highest expression of concern for patient care. But quickly and inevitably it becomes focused on cost containment at the expense of patient care.[76]

Because we live in a world of limited resources even for obviously good things, governments that have taken charge of health systems soon come to view the sick not as people to be helped, but as costs to be minimized. Harvard Business School professor, Regina Herzlinger, tells us that, "The truly sick constitute only 20 percent of health-care users, but account for 80 percent of health-care costs." This makes the sick "a politically vulnerable target for cost control through rationing."[77] An economy can only devote so much of its wealth to health care. There are only so many hospital beds and a finite number of doctors.

My father lives in Canada. He's 74 and he needs a double hip replacement. If he were an American living in America, he would just get them done. But he's a Canadian living in Ontario where the government runs health care, and so also controls health care costs. Thus, Ontario doctors are limited in the number of hip replacements they are allowed to do, producing long waiting lists. So my dad has to wait at least six months for each hip. That's a lot of pain and a big chunk of an old man's life. He's in discussion with doctors in Michigan.

Of course, the pressure to free up beds and reduce costs is intense when dealing with the elderly, but especially with those who appear to be in the final stages of life. The concern not to over-treat is laudable, but a system that doesn't address patients as paying customers will, in its efforts to manage costs and minimize overtreatment, inevitably err in the opposite direction. It will undertreat people who would otherwise survive and recover. For this reason, what Sarah Palin called "death panels" or what advocates called end-of-life-counseling came up during the debate over how to pay for the Democratic health care plan.[78] The provision was dropped from the bill, only to re-emerge as a Medicare regulation just weeks after the law's passage.[79]

Advocates of socialized medicine argue that your health and even your life should not depend on how much money you have. In her section of this chapter, Lisa puts it provocatively: "In the U.S. the right to live is earned through economic fortune or white-collar work. Life is not, in practice, an intrinsic right; the right to live is bought—at a high price." But in the real world, the alternative to price-based rationing is not all the best health care for whoever wants it whenever and wherever. More clinics than JiffyLubes! (Are people not more important than cars?) No appointment necessary. CAT scans in northern Alaska! Premier cancer treatment in the poorest communities! No, that's dreamland. Under the government- controlled alternative in a world of limited resources, your health and even your life depend on box-checking, budget conscious bureaucrats.

Sir Michael Rawlins, chairman of Britain's National Institute for Health and Clinical Excellence (NICE) which decides whether or not the National Health Service will pay for a treatment, is quite blunt, even coldly actuarial, about the necessity of balancing costs and lives:

> All health-care systems are facing the problem of finite resources and almost infinite demand. And all health-care systems have implicitly if not explicitly adopted some form of cost control. In the U.S. you do it by not providing health care to some people. We are best known [for looking] at a new drug, device or diagnostic technique to see whether the increment in the cost of that treatment is worth the increment in the health gain.[80]

Life is full of cost control questions. We face them when we choose a restaurant, make the family budget, and balance the cost of co-pays and deductibles against the value of a medical procedure. ("That tooth will be okay for now without a crown.") When we make tradeoffs to contain personal costs, we make judgments regarding what we see as our overall personal well-being.

A state-run health system, however, does not love you as you love yourself, nor even as your family loves you. So they have to make calculations of "quality-adjusted life years," and decide whether your heart transplant or hip replacement and the "quality of life" you will get from it is worth the public expense. NICE puts the price tag for a year of life in perfect health at $45,000. Thus, life in your golden years is worth a fraction of that...as they see it.[81]

Sarah Palin was right on this point, and on the side of the most helpless among us.[82] Citing economist Thomas Sowell,[83] she warned, "Government health care will not reduce the cost; it will simply refuse to pay the cost. And who will suffer the most when they ration care? The sick, the elderly, and the disabled, of course." Dispersing the decision-making power into the hands of consumers—patients and those closest to them—is on balance the safest and most humane alternative.

CARING FOR THE HELPLESS

What about those who are desperately short in their ability to pay? We can help the poorest among us in less bureaucratically compromised ways, such as by families, religious communities, pro bono work by doctors themselves, and private charities.

Americans are quite generous and have a long history of establishing and funding effective ministries and organizations for addressing neighbor-needs. They feed and clothe and bind up wounds at home and at the ends of the earth. They do this through everything from church basements to the Salvation Army and from missionaries to Mercy Ships.

Some think of charity as a ridiculously inadequate answer to the problem of providing the poor with health care. But we underestimate the power and provision of private charitable giving because it is constrained by how much government takes in taxes and it is discouraged by how much government intrudes with entitlements.[84]

Based on what we see today, it is safe to say that in a consumer-driven system hospitals would serve the sick, both rich and poor, with a pricing system similar to what we see in private colleges and universities. In higher education, students from wealthy families pay full fare, while poor kids get a free ride. Donors make up the difference, whether from gratitude for their own education, commitment to the school's mission, or desire to exploit tax breaks. Can we trust doctors and hospitals not to take a "pay up or die" attitude to the sick? Of course we can. The story of Nikki that Lisa shares in her chapter provides an example:

> Thomas W. Green Jr., an internist who coordinated her care, says, 'The whole hospital got very, very emotionally involved with this girl and this family. She didn't give up. They didn't give

> up. There were minor, major miracles, major setbacks.' The hospital kept going even though Ms. White had no insurance. Bristol Regional spent about $900,000 on Ms. White's care. Her tab was one of the nonprofit hospital's largest charity cases that year. In all, it wrote off nearly $19 million in 2006. 'We spent a lot of money on this girl and nobody complained about it,' Dr. Green says.[85]

Our American culture of compassion and mutual respect would prevent private health care providers from taking a strictly commercial approach to their profession.

When the Democrats secured the last vote needed to pass the bill they cobbled together, Sen. Chris Dodd proclaimed, "We stand ready to pass a bill into law that finally makes quality health care a right for every American, not a privilege."

But when any service becomes a "right" from the government instead of a "good" to be purchased, you can expect its management to be politicized, its consumers to be impoverished, and its development to be stunted. Misery of one sort or another inevitably follows when you use something for a purpose contrary to God's design for it. God instituted government to punish evil and praise what is good (I Peter 2:14), not as an instrument for providing all manner of human goods from schooling and health care to opera companies and baseball stadiums.

Democratic health care reform, like much of what the Democrats want to do with government, goes far beyond what I argue God intends government to do. They try to accomplish with government (preferably the federal government) what is properly a private responsibility. They try to shrink the sphere of private liberty by expanding the sphere of public action. What the supporters of this project call compassion or social justice, George Will calls "the dependency agenda."[86] But God tells us that it is the government's job to protect that sphere, not absorb it, so that people can provide for themselves and for one another (I Tim. 2:1-

2). As usual, what is best on every level is liberty, personal responsibility, and generous charity, three traditions that are uniquely Christian and historically American.

IN THE BEGINNING

ON ABORTION

ON ABORTION

D.C. INNES

> "One night, a nursing co-worker was taking an aborted Down's syndrome baby who was born alive to our Soiled Utility Room because his parents did not want to hold him, and she did not have time to hold him. I could not bear the thought of this suffering child dying alone in a Soiled Utility Room, so I cradled and rocked him for the 45 minutes that he lived. He was 21 to 22 weeks old, weighed about ½ pound, and was about 10 inches long. He was too weak to move very much, expending any energy he had trying to breathe. Toward the end, he was so quiet that I couldn't tell if he was still alive unless I held him up to the light to see if his heart was still beating through his chest wall. After he was pronounced dead, we folded his little arms across his chest, wrapped him in a tiny shroud, and carried him to the hospital morgue where all of our dead patients are taken." – Testimony of Jill L. Stanek, RN, at the hearing on the "Born Alive Infant Protection Act of 2000". [87]

It is government's most basic responsibility to protect the helpless. Of course, government exists because everyone is vulnerable to one degree or another, and so government owes protection to everyone under its dominion. If we were fully capable of protecting ourselves and our families from muggers, murderers, rapists, and marauders, God would not have provided and sanctioned the coercive authority of civil government (Romans 13).

But in this protective role, government has a special responsibility to the most helpless precisely on account of their helplessness, those who have nowhere else to turn for their security, those who are uniquely and by the very nature of their circumstances exposed to the whims and designs of the more powerful who would plunder and even kill them for selfish gain.

No one is more helpless than the baby in the womb. This little one is unseen, faceless, nameless. He or she is entirely in the care of the mother, and if the mother's heart becomes murderous, the government must step in with protection. For most of the gestation period, the baby's humanity is indisputable. There is debate over the first stages, but, given that debate, government should err on the side of caution, and protect the dependent life that has begun.[88]

THE EVANGELICAL RECORD

Evangelicals were slow to pick up on abortion as a serious moral issue. Susan Friend Harding gives us a picture of where the Evangelical community stood on abortion during the *Roe* era.

> In 1968, an institute run by *Christianity Today*, the leading Evangelical magazine, organized a symposium on the subject of birth control and abortion. A variety of positions were aired, but the official publication of the symposium affirmed the principle that "the Christian physician will advise induced abortion only to safeguard greater values sanctioned by Scripture. These values should include individual health, family welfare, and social responsibility." A special issue of *Eternity* magazine on abortion in 1971 still presented a range of opinions on the circumstances under which abortions might be advised.[89]

It was not abortion but efforts by the federal government in 1975 to strip Bob Jones University of its tax-exempt status on account of its segregationist policies that initially spurred Evangelicals to engage politics. At the Moral Majority's founding in 1979, abortion was something of an afterthought.[90] It was not *Roe v. Wade* in 1973, but Dr. C. Everett Koop and Francis Schaeffer in 1979 that drew Evangelicals together on the abortion issue.[91] Koop and Schaeffer sounded the alarm and awakened the Protestant Christian conscience with their book and subsequent film, *Whatever Happened to the Human Race?* Again, as Harding tells us, "The film established the framework within which opposition to abortion rights came to be understood as the modal [sic.], 'traditional' Christian position." [92]

Despite Evangelicals' less than admirable response to the *Roe* decision, in time they did respond, and with great energy and conviction. The Pro-Life stance became as synonymous with being Evangelical as it had once been with being Catholic, and their firmness on the issue together with their place in the Reagan coalition pulled the Republican Party into official opposition to the practice.

THE REPUBLICAN RECORD

Since Evangelicals joined the Republican governing coalition *en masse* in 1980, the GOP has clearly distinguished itself by its efforts, in both word and deed, to protect our unborn children against death by abortion. President Ronald Reagan fully embraced the Evangelical position opposing abortion, and he used his bully pulpit to keep the moral question stirred up in popular debate and to lend the weight of his office to one side. In 1983, he wrote *Abortion and the Conscience of the Nation*, originally an unsolicited article for *The Human Life Review* on the occasion of the tenth anniversary of *Roe v. Wade*.[93] In it, he called the nation to a deeper cultural attitude of concern for innocent life: "We cannot diminish the value of one category of human life—the unborn—without diminishing the value of all human life." Republican President, George W. Bush, has been no less vocal in his support for innocent life in the womb. In his third debate with John Kerry in 2004, he defended "a culture of life" and tried to find common ground with Democrats in opposing unambiguous evils, like partial-birth abortion, and promoting obvious goods, like adoption.

> It's important to promote a culture of life. A hospitable society is a society where every being counts and every person matters. The ideal world is one in which every child is protected in law and welcomed to life. I understand there's great differences [sic] on this issue of abortion, but I believe reasonable people can come together and put good law in place that will help reduce the number of abortions.[94]

When it comes to the American presidency, there is no such thing as mere words. Presidential rhetoric has the power to shape the attitude of a generation.

Republican defense of children in the womb has gone well beyond rhetoric, however. In 1976, shortly after the Roe decision, Congress passed the Hyde Amendment, introduced by Illinois Republican Congressman, Henry Hyde, which prohibited the federal government spending money (largely Medicaid) on abortion except when the pregnancy endangered the mother's life. Congress has attached the amendment to the annual appropriations bill for the Department of Health and Human Services each year since 1977, from time to time adding or removing restrictions such as exceptions for cases of rape and incest.

In 1983, Utah Republican Senator, Orrin Hatch, supported by Roman Catholic Democrat Thomas Eagleton of Missouri, introduced a constitutional amendment stating simply, "A right to abortion is not secured by this Constitution." It failed, 49-50 (needing 60 votes to pass), under heavy opposition largely by Democrats. That was the high water mark of legislative attempts to overturn *Roe v. Wade*.

Naturally, attempts to overturn Roe have been judicial as well, and they continue to this day. While the Democratic record on Supreme Court nominees has been consistently liberal on abortion, the Republican record over the last 30 years has been mixed, albeit unintentionally for the most part. Reagan's first pick, Sandra Day O'Connor, infuriated conservatives and her judgments were no help to the unborn. By contrast, Justices Scalia, Thomas, Roberts, and Alito have faithfully refused to bend the constitution to suit the abortion agenda for which it was never intended. Justice Anthony Kennedy, Reagan's second choice after the more impressive Robert Bork was politicked into defeat, has been inconsistent, and David Souter, the quiet bachelor from New Hampshire, was a profound disappointment to George H. W. Bush who appointed him.

In 1984, Reagan signed an executive order instituting what came to be known as the Mexico City policy requiring that non-governmental organizations "'neither perform nor actively promote abortion as a method of family planning in other nations" if they wish to receive U.S. funds. His successor in office, George H. W. Bush, continued it, but one of Democrat Bill Clinton's first acts as President was to rescind it. George W. Bush reinstituted it, and Democratic President Obama was swift to repeal it again when he took office.[95]

While constitutional law on abortion and its circumstances has moved back and forth for the last third of a century depending on the philosophical balance of the court between liberals and conservatives, the practice of abortion has advanced to monstrous new extremes: partial-birth abortion and the harvesting of living aborted babies for medical research. To confront these new evils, President George W. Bush signed the Partial-Birth Abortion Ban Act of 2003, and vetoed the Stem Cell Research Enhancement Act in 2006 and again in 2007, two of his rare vetoes.[96] He also appointed the President's Council on Bioethics in 2001 that produced a morally serious defense of human dignity. While many members of the Council were not Christians, e.g. Leon Kass, the conclusions resonated with the Christian ethical tradition.[97]

THE DEMOCRATIC RECORD

Since 1973, Democrats have gone beyond a mere defense of a woman's right to an abortion to supporting an ever-widening range of abortion options and opposing even the mildest restrictions. The justification they offer is that any restriction at all would threaten to undermine *Roe v Wade*. When Justice Breyer wrote for the court in striking down a Nebraska law forbidding partial-birth abortion, he cited, "an undue burden upon a woman's right to make an abortion decision."[98] When the high court upheld the 2003 Partial Birth Abortion Ban Act, Clinton appointee Justice Ruth Bader Ginsburg wrote in her dissent that the majority opinion in that case "cannot be understood as anything other than an effort to chip away a right declared again and again by this court, and with increasing comprehension of its centrality to women's lives."[99]

Beginning in 1976, the Supreme Court has struck down state laws requiring the husband's consent or that of the parents in the case of a minor,[100] waiting periods after receiving information about abortion,[101] that second and third trimester abortions be done in a hospital,[102] and that women seeking abortions be given detailed information about the process.[103] Elected Democrats, such as Presidents Bill Clinton and Barack Obama, appoint and support judges that decide cases this way, whereas Republicans overwhelmingly oppose them in the nomination and confirmation process.

As early as 1992, Bill Clinton, as presidential candidate, said he wanted to keep abortion safe, legal, and rare.[104] But when it came to rarity, his deeds sharply contradicted his words. Upon taking office in 1993, President Bill Clinton 1) rescinded the Title 10 "gag rule" on abortion counseling at federally funded family planning clinics,[105] 2) repealed the Mexico City Policy,[106] 3) repealed the ban on funding fetal tissue transplants,[107] 4) permitted military hospitals to provide privately funded abortion services,[108] and 5) reviewed the ban on the French abortion drug, RU-486, the so-called morning after pill.[109] In 1996, he vetoed the Partial-Birth Abortion Ban Act passed by Congress the previous year. Firm in what he did, he vetoed it again in 1997.[110]

Matters have only become worse under our most recent Democratic president. In 2008, Princeton's Robert George called Barack Obama "the most extreme pro-abortion candidate ever to seek the office of President of the United States" and "the most extreme pro-abortion legislator ever to serve in either house of the United States Congress."[111] Not only does he oppose any ban on partial-birth abortion, he goes beyond even that.

When it became known that babies who survived abortion attempts were being left to die—even, as noted before, being tossed into a soiled-linen closet—legislators from across the abortion divide united to require humane care in those circumstances, regardless of the infant's long-term viability. The federal bill passed 98-0 in the Senate.

Barack Obama, however, as Illinois state senator, opposed the Illinois version of the bill, even though it was virtually identical to the federal version. He was the only member to speak against it.[112] His fear? Speaking on the Illinois Senate floor in 2001, he argued that, "[I]t would essentially ban abortions, because the equal protection clause does not allow somebody to kill a child, and if this is a child, then this would be an antiabortion statute."[113] Not even Democrats in the United States Senate shared his fear to such a radical extent: withholding protection even from an infant abortion survivor out of fear that it might somehow threaten abortion rights.

Nevertheless, the depth of support in the Democratic Party for partial-birth abortion illustrates dramatically how devoted the party is to the practice of abortion in all its forms, at every stage of pregnancy, and, in some cases, even beyond. The horror of the practice is clear to everyone but the most ideologically hardened and spiritually blinded.

Consider precisely what partial-birth abortion is:

> The further along a pregnancy is, the more complicated—and the more controversial—the procedures are for aborting it. Abortions performed after the 20th week of pregnancy typically require that the fetus be dismembered inside the womb so it can be removed without damaging the pregnant woman's cervix.

> Some gynecologists consider such methods, known as "dilation and evacuation" [D&E] less than ideal because they can involve substantial blood loss and may increase the risk of lacerating the cervix, potentially undermining the woman's ability to bear children in the future. Two abortion physicians, one in Ohio and one in California, independently developed variations on the method by extracting the fetus intact. The Ohio physician, Martin Haskell, called his method "dilation and extraction," or D&X. It involved dilating the woman's cervix, then pulling the fetus through it feet first until only the head remained inside. Using scissors or another sharp instrument, the head was then punctured, and the skull compressed, so it, too, could fit through the dilated cervix.[114]

According to the pro-abortion Alan Guttmacher Institute, of the 1.3 million abortions performed in the year 2000, 15,000 occurred after the woman's 20th week, almost all of them between weeks 20 and 24. (A pregnancy lasts 40 weeks.) Of those, doctors used the D&X, or partial-birth, method in only about 2,200 abortions, or in 0.17 percent of the procedures performed annually.[115] That is what advocates of partial birth abortion are fighting to defend.

Those who defend the procedure are essentially "fencing the law," as the Pharisees of old used to say. To prevent a slippery slope, they draw far back from the crest of the hill. If Congress bans D&X, surely D&E will be next, as its description is just as emotionally unsettling. Restricting even the most morally radical practice of abortion would move the country in the direction of banning all abortions. Partial birth abortions are rare and gruesome and obviously murderous. Nonetheless, despite this, and despite polling that indicates sixty-nine percent of Americans oppose the procedure,[116] there remains a significant bloc of Democratic officeholders who defend it with moral passion.

God is the author of life. Knowing Him in Christ is fullness of life. Where his presence is, there is life. Where he withdraws, there is death. When people deny God, they deny life. The God-denying Soviet Communists killed tens of millions of their own citizens. The atheistic government in communist China, as part of their one-child policy, forces mothers to abort their unborn children. In America, our cultural and political authorities have been turning away from God for the last 40 years, and, as a consequence, we have tolerated and even encouraged 50 million abortions since 1973.[117] Our loss has been the equivalent of a self-inflicted nuclear strike.

Sin carries with it natural as well as divine consequences. A nation that kills its young will itself perish.

LISA SHARON HARPER

I believe life begins before conception. It begins in the mind of God, who is the author of life. God dreams of us before we're conceived, watches us in our mothers' wombs, knows every hair on our heads and every day ordained for our lives before even one is lived. Thus, to abort a pregnancy is an affront against God. It breaks relationship with God because it declares to God, "I do not trust you or your ways — the ways of love and life and faith." It breaks the relationship between parent and child, and more, it breaks the relationship between the child and her very life.

I also believe sin is sin is sin. According to the scriptures, murderers, fornicators, liars, drunkards, and slave traders are all law-breakers in need of a savior.[118] Abortion, the termination of a life before it has had the chance to live, is no more of a sin than lying and no less a sin than murder. And Jesus died to forgive and redeem them all. Jesus' blood on the cross and his resurrection from the dead are enough. Jesus is enough.

David declares that the state carries the basic obligation to protect its people. I agree. Yet this is where we part ways. He assumes our government should support the specific mandates of the Christian faith. But in the eyes of our Constitution, no one set of religious beliefs trumps any other. Rather, it is good and right that our faith moves us to action in the public square, but it cannot be the sole basis of our argument once we get there. In our pluralistic society I am obligated to win the public argument based on common values and credible evidence. Thus, any religious definition of the beginning of life cannot be the criteria used to decide at what point gestation becomes 'life'. Constitutionally, the cornerstone of the Supreme Court's decision in the landmark case, Roe v. Wade, hangs on this fact.

ROE V. WADE

In September 1969, Norma L. McCorvey, single and the product of a troubled family, discovered she was pregnant with her third child. In Texas her only legal option was to carry the baby to term. Determined to get an abortion, McCorvey fabricated a story that she had been raped, which provided an exception to Texas' strict abortion prohibition. Due to lack of police evidence, the rape charge fell moot. McCorvey sought an illegal abortion, but couldn't secure one. So she sued Dallas County District Attorney, Henry Wade, for the right to abort and went down in annuls of history as Jane Roe.[119] The case went to the Supreme Court.

The court's judgment rested on two major points: 1) a woman's constitutional right to exercise "liberty" (dominion) over her own body is "a fundamental right" protected by the liberty clause in the Fourteenth Amendment, which states, "nor shall any State deprive any person of life, liberty, or property." This is where the slogan "a woman's right to choose" comes from. It is her civil right to exercise agency over her own body. But the court added a key caveat: in the case of pregnancy, a woman's right to exercise dominion over her body is not absolute. It is subject to limitations; namely the States' inherent interest in the protection of prenatal life.[120] The court explained: "If this suggestion of personhood is established, the appellant's case, of course, collapses, for the fetus' right to life would then be guaranteed specifically by the Amendment."[121] Constitutionally, the Fourteenth Amendment protects only "born" persons, but the state still has interests in protecting the potentiality of life, according to the court. Thus, the crux of the court's ruling hinged not on whether one supported life or choice; it hinged on a second question: how does our pluralistic society define when life begins and/or becomes viable?

The court declined to answer the question of what constitutes the beginning of life. Citing diverse historic opinions of philosophers, physicians, church dogma and theologians, the court declared it was not qualified to settle that question. It is noteworthy that if the court had used any one religious measure to settle this question, it would have breached the First Amendment, which is one of the most distinctive gifts of U.S. governance. It guarantees the free exercise of religion and forbids the state from establishing one religion to govern all. If the court had used my faith or David's faith as its measuring stick, it certainly would have found that the baby in the womb is a person worthy of protection by the law. But the court could not use my faith or anyone else's as its ruler. So, it moved to a question that could be settled using the lowest common denominator of knowledge available in a pluralistic society—medicine.

The question of *viability* became the hinge point: at what point in the gestation period can a life survive on its own outside the mother's womb? The court concluded:

> ... the "compelling" point is at viability. This is so because the fetus then presumably has the capability of meaningful life outside the mother's womb. State regulation protective of fetal life after viability thus has both logical and biological justifications. If the State is interested in protecting fetal life after viability, it may go so far as to proscribe abortion [410 U.S. 113, 164] during that period, except when it is necessary to preserve the life or health of the mother.[122]

In other words, the State's interest in and obligation to protect the prenatal life kicks in at the point when the fetus could experience meaningful life on its own outside the mother's womb for an extended amount of time. Before that point, the woman's right to exercise dominion over her own body is fundamentally protected by the Fourteenth Amendment. After the point of viability, the State may opt to forbid abortion in the interest of the child, *except* in cases where the life or health of the mother is at risk. The point of viability is generally accepted to start somewhere between 24 and 28 weeks. The ultimate determination of viability, however, was declared the responsibility of the mother's attending physician.

Randall Balmer, a religious historian and Evangelical Baptist, charts the initial response of the Evangelical church to the *Roe v. Wade* ruling in his book, *Thy Kingdom Come:*

> The vast majority of Evangelical leaders said virtually nothing about it; many of those who did comment actually applauded the decision. W. Barry Garrett of Baptist Press wrote, "Religious liberty, human equality and justice are advanced by the Supreme Court abortion decision." Indeed, even before the *Roe* decision, the messengers (delegates) to the 1971 Southern Baptist Convention gathering in St. Louis, Missouri adopted a resolution that stated, "We call upon Southern Baptists to work for legislation that will allow the possibility of abortion under such conditions as rape, incest, clear evidence of severe fetal deformity, and carefully ascertained evidence of the likelihood of damage to the emotional, mental, and physical health of the mother."[123]

Balmer also cites W.A. Criswell, former president of the Southern Baptist Convention and pastor of First Baptist Church in Dallas, who said, "I have always felt that it was only after a child was born and had life separate from its mother that it became an individual person and it has always, therefore, seemed to me that what is best for the mother and for the future should be allowed."[124]

AWAKENING THE SLEEPING GIANT

So when did the gulf occur between the Evangelical response to *Roe v. Wade* then and its current position? During the mid-1970s to the mid-1990s, Balmer reveals and my co-author rightly acknowledges that the Religious Right was formed in defense of Bob Jones University's 1975 fight to retain its tax-exempt status while maintaining racist admission policies. These policies first prohibited African Americans from admission, then prohibited single African Americans from admission, then prohibited the practice or support of interracial dating. But this is not the narrative known by most Evangelicals. According to the traditional narrative, the Roe v. Wade ruling rallied the masses, awaking the sleeping Evangelical giant. This is a myth. What actually woke the giant? Evangelical leaders were threatened by the dismantling of racist institutions, not *Roe v. Wade*.[125]

And there is another myth masquerading as truth in the halls of Evangelical churches and institutions: that overturning *Roe v. Wade* would outlaw abortion. It would not.

Before the *Roe v. Wade* ruling, there was no federal legal standard over the practice or prohibition of abortion. Women and the unborn were both subject to the whims of their state courts and legislatures. The *Roe v. Wade* ruling offered, for the first time in U.S. history, a federal legal standard over the practice and prohibition of abortion.

If the Religious Right had its way and the *Roe* ruling were overturned, abortion would not be outlawed. Rather, the legislative power over abortion law would be handed back to the individual states, and anti- abortion advocates would have to adopt a fifty-state strategy to outlaw abortion effectively in the U.S. As passionate as the movement is, such a fight would require an unrealistic measure of resources and time.

What's more, the states most likely to outlaw abortion already have the lowest abortion rates: Missouri, South Dakota, Kentucky, Mississippi, Idaho, and Utah all have abortion rates of less than 8 per 1000 women.

States like New York, California, Delaware, Rhode Island, Nevada, and Massachusetts, among others, all have abortion rates of more than 18 per 1000 women—with one as high as 30 per 1000.[126] These solidly Democratic states are least likely to outlaw abortion given the opportunity. So, in a very practical sense, the fifty- state strategy would do next to nothing to lower the number of actual lives being aborted in the U.S. annually.

Even the Republican Party recognizes the fifty-state strategy is not a viable option. Balmer points out that during the Bush presidency, from 2003 to 2006, Republicans controlled both houses of Congress and the Executive Office of government and yet, during that period, not one measure was put forward to outlaw the practice of abortion.

David mentioned the "Partial-Birth Abortion Ban Act of 2003"; it's important to note that the ban *was not* a measure to outlaw abortion. It prohibited a particular kind of abortion procedure called "intact dilation and extraction." My coauthor decried the audacity of the Democratic Party for its round revolt against the ban—Clinton vetoed two attempts to pass the Ban during his presidency and few Democrats voted in favor of the ban when it was passed in 2003. David asks how could the Democrats be so heartless? Because, as crafted by the Republican Party, the legislation is heartless toward the health and very lives of mothers. President Clinton explained in his veto declaration: "The bill does not allow women to protect themselves from serious threats to their health. By refusing to permit women, in reliance on their doctors' best medical judgment, to use their [sic] procedure when their lives are threatened or when their health is put in serious jeopardy, the Congress has fashioned a bill that is consistent neither with the Constitution nor with sound public policy."[127] Likewise, when the ban's constitutionality was challenged in the Supreme Court case *Gonzales v. Carhart*, the court split down ideological lines in favor of the ban by the slimmest of margins, 5-4. The dissenting opinion written by Justice Ruth Ginsburg read:

> Today's decision is alarming...It tolerates, indeed applauds, federal intervention to ban nationwide a procedure found necessary and proper in certain cases by the American College of Obstetricians and Gynecologists (ACOG). It blurs the line, firmly drawn in *Casey*, between previability and postviability abortions. And, for the first time since *Roe*, the Court blesses a prohibition with no exception safeguarding a woman's health.[128]

And what was the effect of the ban? It did nothing to outlaw abortion itself or to lower actual abortion rates. Only .17 percent of all abortions were partial birth abortions in 2000.[129] Yet, the ban has increased the health risks of pregnant women across the United States.

So, if overturning *Roe v. Wade* and the fifty-state strategy aren't viable, then what strategy actually works to save unborn lives? Lives are saved when we address abortion for what it is: a poverty issue. Poverty preys on women and children.

The Guttmacher Institute is an official Collaborating Center for the United Nations World Health Organization. In May 2010 the Institute issued a report warning that abortion has become more concentrated among poor women in the U.S. "The proportion of abortion patients who were poor jumped by 60 percent in 2008," according to the report. Eighty-five percent of women having abortions were unmarried and "the abortion rate for low-income women was three times that of better-off women."[130]

ABORTION RATES DROP

Couple this information with one stark fact: we have had five Republican presidents and three Democratic presidents since the Roe ruling. Which president saw the steepest drop in abortion rates on his watch? President Bill Clinton—a solid five percentage points, a virtual abortion rate nosedive. How is that possible? President Clinton dramatically increased funding for effective programs that help women and children and it worked. Programs like State Children's Health Insurance Program

(SCHIP), Welfare reform, Women with Infants and Children (WIC), Food Stamps, and Head Start helped mothers exercise their dominion in ways that helped preserve the relationships between mothers and God, mothers and their children, and children and their very lives.

President Obama's Health Reform law will help tens of millions more women to choose life. Wall Street reforms passed by the Democratic 111th Congress and signed into law by President Obama will help millions to avoid the slippery slope of credit card debt that traps so many in deep wells of poverty. Likewise, the Lilly Ledbetter Fair Pay Act will finally give women the right to earn equal pay as their male counterparts; again increasing women's ability to choose life.

Republican leaders in the 112th Congress have vowed to repeal each of these gains and to balance the U.S. budget on the backs of poor mothers; slashing funding for programs like Food Stamps, WIC, and Head Start. With these vows they have, in effect, promised to place obstacles in the paths of mothers who might otherwise choose life.

There is a growing chorus of Evangelicals working across the aisle to find practical ways to lower the number of abortions in the U.S. each year. The mantra of this choir is simple: Political ideology doesn't matter. What matters is what works to help families choose life and live that life more abundantly.

I am a member of that choir. I reject the manipulative and artificial dividing line between "Pro-life" and "Pro-choice." As this is a line drawn by political strategists, not by Jesus. It was drawn for one purpose—not to save lives, not to build the Kingdom of God, but to move the hands of Evangelicals in the voting booth. But this is an unwinnable war and I reject its battle cry. In this "culture war" everyone loses—especially the ones we claim to fight for—the unborn. No. My faith calls me to support the protection of all life, including the mothers', and to call for a consistent ethic of life, one that rejects all public policy that effectively breaks *shalom* by fracturing families and ending viable lives.

THE TWO SHALL BE ONE

ON SAME-SEX MARRIAGE

ON SAME-SEX MARRIAGE

D.C. INNES

Why are Evangelicals upset with public acceptance of homosexuality? They are not busybodies looking to meddle in other people's business, though some may be. Nor is the issue simply a matter of establishing philosophical or theological truths, though it's clearly important to settle those. What drives Evangelicals is the need to defend family and the faith. Legally accepting homosexual relationships as marriages would fundamentally change our understanding of the nature and purpose of marriage, and would therefore turn marriages sharply in a socially destructive direction. At stake in this matter are the blessings that a healthy society brings not only to people in general, but also to the church which has the inherently difficult task of making disciples of its children.

THE LATEST BATTLE AND THE LARGER WAR

The question of same-sex marriage is best viewed in the context of the culture wars of the last fifty years that includes a history of cultural breakdown and a broad assault on the Christian faith and family. In 1979, Jerry Falwell formed the Moral Majority. This launch of a Baptist minister into the political fray marked a turning point in American politics. Evangelicals had disengaged from political and social issues since the Scopes trial in the 1920s. They turned inward to "preach, pray, and practice," leaving the world to itself. But by the 1960s and 1970s, they found government and culture intruding destructively on the Christian family and the ability of Christians to raise their children in godliness. In the mid-seventies, Evangelicals re-emerged in public life as they came to realize that the family was under increasing strain from corrosive political and cultural forces.

At that time, the culture war was already at a fierce pitch. In 1962, the Supreme Court declared school prayer unconstitutional.[131] For Christians, the issue was not just religious utterances during opening exercises. At stake was the secularization of six intensely instructive hours in every child's weekday.

The rest of the swinging sixties gave us not only the drug culture but also the sexual revolution. In 1972, the Supreme Court made "the pill" easily available to unmarried women.[132] That same year, the Equal Rights Amendment passed both houses of Congress, but Conservative Evangelicals saw it as a constitutionalization of feminism and an assault on the Christian fabric of society. In January of the next year, *Roe v. Wade* gave first-trimester abortion the nobility of a constitutionally-protected right.

At the same time, gay liberation was challenging conventional understandings of wholesome sexuality. If gay were to become part of "the new normal," then home and church would be in constant battle against the culturally-accepted standards of family and sexual conduct. There has always been immorality, but it has always been recognized as...immorality.

After the Moral Majority came the Christian Coalition, and then a secular recognition of "values voters." Despite all this powerful organizing and three sympathetic presidents, there has been little progress on the culture front.[133] After decades of skirmishing over public religious expression, the nation's major cultural institutions are thoroughly secularized. The Equal Rights Amendment failed, but feminist egalitarianism is now our cultural default. As for abortion, not only did Evangelicals fail to overturn *Roe v. Wade*, we are now fighting to stop what may reasonably be termed "point-of-birth infanticide." Whereas homosexuals once pressed for open participation in society, they are now on the verge of full affirmation through acceptance of same-sex marriage arrangements.

WHO IS ON THE FAMILY'S SIDE?

The Democratic Party has actively supported the normalization of homosexuality ever since it broke ground by adding "sexual orientation" to the anti-discrimination plank of their party platform in 1980.[134]

Most recently, in a White House ceremony, President Obama recognized homosexuality as not only morally acceptable, but even praiseworthy, proclaiming June 2010 to be Lesbian, Gay, Bisexual, and Transgender Pride Month. "This month, as we recognize the immeasurable contributions of LGBT Americans, we renew our commitment to the struggle for equal rights for LGBT Americans and to ending prejudice and injustice wherever it exists."[135] Normalization was clearly his goal when he said, "They are our mothers and fathers, our sons and daughters, and our friends and neighbors. Across my Administration, openly LGBT employees are serving at every level." He identified that normalization with "a more perfect union." Obama says he does not support recognizing same-sex unions as marriages, but when he said, "we must give committed gay couples the same rights and responsibilities afforded to any married couple, and repeal the Defense of Marriage Act," it is hard to distinguish that from presidential support for same-sex marriage. Since then, he has described his view regarding same-sex marriage as "evolving."[136] In February of 2011, he instructed his justice department to stop defending the Defense of Marriage Act in court, calling it "unconstitutional."[137]

Just a decade ago, suggesting that Democrats would eventually support gay marriage was considered a ridiculous and fear-mongering slur against their party. Nevertheless, that is now the default position of enlightened Democrats. In a 2010 poll, support for same-sex marriage among Democrats was 56 percent, thirty-seven points higher than among Republicans.[138]

THE FAMILY IS FUNDAMENTAL

Redefining the nature of the family, however, is like trying to restructure the human body. No good can come of it. Underlying every good that we derive from society—safety, trust, learning, prosperity, chastity, and countless others—is the proper understanding and functioning of the family. Where family structure and authority weaken or disintegrate, these goods melt away. That's why God instituted not just reproduction, but specifically marriage. He sanctified it for his people and protected it with laws.

Edmund Burke, the philosopher of modern conservatism, calls families "little platoons."[139] The attachments formed in a small natural society like the family lift people, he says, outside of their self- satisfying, self-exalting concerns and cultivate the more widely-cast affections like love of country and respect for neighbor.

> "To be attached to the subdivision, to love the little platoon we belong to in society, is the first principle (the germ as it were) of public affections. It is the first link in the series by which we proceed toward a love to our country and to mankind."

These platoons make war on the enemy of peace that dwells by nature in the human heart. The family is the battlefront where selfish little monster-pups develop into responsible, considerate, productive adults. Moms and dads—married couples—plan the campaign, lead the charge, and do most of the fighting. They do it for free and they do it in love. There is no substitute for them. Wise political leaders, therefore, are vigilant in protecting the family and mindful that government programs, though perhaps well-intentioned, do not undermine it. Unwise leaders, for example, gave us family-destroying programs such as Aid to Families with Dependent Children, the welfare law that penalized intact two-parent families, favoring single moms instead.

God gives children to parents with the mandate to raise them "in the fear and admonition of the Lord." (Eph. 6:4) While local evangelism and foreign missions are part of God's design for the church's growth, the primary means by which the Christian faith passes from one generation to the next is the Christian family.

Parents live out their faith under their children's daily watch. But it doesn't start there. Christian men and women marry one another. Then they have children. They school those children in the disciplines of self-government and self-giving. And they teach the faith. Children learn the doctrine of sin, but by the hard experience of transgression and rebuke, they also learn they are themselves sinners. Through the hugs of reconciliation that follow the tears of red-bottomed remorse, they learn that God is not only holy; He is gracious. And in these teachable moments, wise Christian parents point their children to the gracious Savior. The cultural assault on the family that we see today, therefore, is an assault on the Christian faith.

But extending marriage to homosexuals destroys marriage for everyone. If two men can marry, or two women, what exactly is marriage? Is marriage just close friendship between any two people? Is it the solemnization of any two best friends in a sexual relationship?[140] What's solemn about that? Is the solemnity in the permanence of it? Surely it is people's own business how long they want to remain friends and intimate. Why is the state involved? Why is the church involved? Why are there weddings at all?

Same-sex marriage suggests all of these questions because it is a relationship that, in principle, has nothing to do with the begetting and moral formation of the next generation on which all of life depends. It is just two people indulging themselves together for the time being. We have weddings as community events because every marriage, God willing, is the community's lifeline to the future. It's how we beget and train the next generation. The community has a stake in the permanence and health of the marriage.[141] This is not true of homosexual couples by the very nature of the relationship.

If we were to recognize the homosexual relationship as a marriage, then, fundamentally, we would reduce everyone's marriage to essentially that relationship. Sexual complementarity and childbearing would become optional add-ons, not an essential feature and a natural fulfillment. There would be nothing solemn, therefore, about anyone's marriage, and no expectation of permanency. The indiscriminate sale of birth control and our easy divorce laws have already taken a heavy toll on our understanding of marriage, though the old ideas persist because of the nature of the union. But equating homosexual "marriage" with heterosexual marriage destroys the basis for those ideas.

DECIDING THIS MATTER

There are simpler reasons than these for balking at the notion of giving homosexual co-habitation the legal status of marriage. A marriage is a union of people who complement each other. Two men don't do that, whatever their individual personalities may be. Men and women also were made for each other anatomically. The bits are designed by nature's God to fit together. Two women don't work that way. If two men can marry each other, there's no reason that any combination of people in any number can't form a marriage, which is clearly absurd. If all things work well, marriage results in children. By accident of nature, some couples can't have children. But among homosexuals, childlessness is a principle of nature, not an accident. And so on.

But it is not through arguments that moral culture comes into being and sustains itself. The rational justification for a people's moral understandings has to be possible. In the Christian West, we have a rich tradition of moral philosophy and theology. But it is not by such subtle reasoning that a free people settles for itself the moral questions that underlie public policy. They revert instead to four moral foundation stones: religion, tradition, intuition, and revulsion.

First, it is common and good for people to make moral judgments on the basis of their religion, whether for their private lives or for the public life of their community.[142] The Bible is unambiguous on the morality of homosexuality. God made Adam and Eve. Eve was "suitable" for Adam. He made no provision—whether in the garden or in Israel or in the church of Christ—for homosexual pairing. None. Indeed, He calls it an abomination (Lev.18:22). To condone our society dignifying these relationships with the name "marriage" would be to participate in sin. This is obvious.

Second, in moral matters, tradition must carry a lot of weight. If people always and everywhere have rejected something as evil, *viz.* same-sex marriage, there must be a good reason for it, and you don't overturn that judgment without overwhelming moral counterweight. But the moral innovators of our day recognize no such wisdom. They celebrate themselves as rebels, pioneers, and visionaries simply for shattering moral norms. When sitcom character Murphy Brown happily chose to start a single mother family when she conceived a child out of wedlock, liberals mocked Vice-president Dan Quayle for his reservations.[143] Later, the National Center for Health Statistics confirmed what should have been obvious to everyone.[144]

Third, the intuition of what we call common sense plays a large and legitimate role in shaping and sustaining moral culture. Moral intuition is where the intellectuals' arguments appear in people's peripheral vision, as it were. Insofar as people are not cowed and desensitized by a bombardment of heartrending tales of bullied teenagers, carefully crafted situation comedies, or kissing couples on the evening news, married men and women sense that two men sharing their bodies and a mailing address is not the same as what we have always called marriage. The insights of psychology (before it was politicized), philosophy, and biology (though the arrangement of body parts is hardly an insight) strike most people as obvious once they're stated.

Finally, people who are raised in healthy religion and traditions and who are thus equipped with properly functioning moral intuitions feel revulsion at what is morally appalling. In 2010, Columbia University political science professor David Epstein was discovered to have been having a three-year incestuous though consensual relationship with his 24-year-old daughter. According to reports, they "often exchanged twisted text messages."[145] It is right to be repulsed at this thought. To react any other way would reflect poorly on you. The fact that these two people are consenting adults has nothing to do with the moral status of their relationship.

The prophet Jeremiah describes people whose religion and culture are corrupt and whose moral sensibilities are deadened. "Were they ashamed when they committed abomination? No, they were not at all ashamed; they did not know how to blush" (Jer. 6:15). When we can no longer feel revulsion at these moral abominations, we will be deaf even to the best intellectual arguments against them. Bereft of any substantive moral discernment, we will see no choice but to leave each man to do what is right in his own sight. That is precisely what the political and cultural left is fighting to establish today, and that is also why they are fighting to establish it.

In other words, ordinary people sense that "it's not the same," "it's not actually a marriage," and that to call homosexual co-habitation "marriage" diminishes the meaning of their own marriages. There are other moral evils that diminish marriage as well—easy divorce, adultery, physical abuse, just to name a few. But most of those are recognized as evil. We don't enshrine them in law.

It is tempting to sidestep this contentious issue of open homosexuality and what we do with it as a people by bracketing the moral question, and viewing it as simply an issue of equal protection of the law. That position would hold that, regardless of their sexual orientation and chosen home life, homosexuals should enjoy the same protections of law as the rest of us. In particular, therefore, they should be able to "marry" each other. But that begs the question whether their relationship can in principle be marriage at all.

Of course, none of this justifies personal cruelty to people who, perhaps through tragic circumstances, are confused in their sexual desires. They are human beings. They are made in the image of God. Like any sinner, they need the love of God's people if they are going to see the gracious way back to the Father through Christ. But justifying and dignifying sin, and calling something marriage that is not, is no way to love a sinner.

LISA SHARON HARPER

It was the run up to the 2004 presidential election when the Republican Party introduced the Federal Marriage Amendment to the U.S. Constitution that would define marriage as solely the union of a man and a woman. At the same time, 11 states introduced similar amendments to their state Constitutions. Senator John Kerry, the Democratic candidate for president, did not support gay marriage, but he opposed the constitutional amendment. Suddenly, the nation was enmeshed in a national debate over the right of gay, lesbian, and bi-sexual people to marry each other. And constitutional amendments in swing states created tapestries of unlikely coalitions; those voters played a significant role in President George Bush's second term election.

The next year, I moved back to New York City after a fourteen-year stint in Los Angeles, to attend Columbia University where I earned a Master's Degree in Human Rights. New York City has the largest gay, lesbian, and bisexual population in the United States, and everywhere I turned I was confronted with the question, "What do you think about gay rights and same-sex marriage?" It came up in conversations with a co-worker at Columbia University Chaplains office who is a gay-rights activist; with friends in my program who are international human rights advocates for gay marriage; with friends in my Evangelical church. It came up in my work with New York Faith and Justice (NYFJ) as we reached out and connected with faith leaders and pastors across the city to eradicate poverty. Likewise, it comes up in my current work with Sojourners as I work to mobilize a national, often tenuous, coalition of Christian faith leaders to address issues of poverty, environmental injustice, and war and peace. If gay marriage fell within the purview of the mission of NY Faith and Justice or Sojourners, I would have been compelled to wrestle with this issue in public. But since it is not, I have only had to wrestle over this relentless question in private—until now.

To be honest, as an Evangelical who values the scripture and justice, this issue has presented me with more biblical, constitutional, and just plain practical conundrums than any other issue addressed in this book. I'm comforted to know I am not alone. Major denominations across the United States are splitting over leaders' positions on the rights of lesbian, gay, bisexual, transgender (LGBT) members to be married and ordained. Likewise, while Republicans were united in their opposition to gay marriage in the run up to the 2004 election, Democrats were split. Years later, the Democratic Party is still, like me, in process over the question. President Obama himself consistently cites his Christian faith when he explains why he supports the institution of civil unions, but not same-sex marriage.

For the purpose of this discussion, then, I will focus on one thing: same-sex marriage and the question of its legalization in the United States of America—not whether homosexual acts are sin or whether same-sex marriages should be sanctioned by the church.

Divorce and remarriage after divorce are clearly sin, according to Jesus. Yet no party is rushing to introduce legislation to outlaw divorce. In fact, according to a 2008 study conducted by George Barna, born again Christians are actually slightly more likely to have experienced a divorce (32 percent) than atheists and agnostics (30 percent).[146] Thus, even by our own standards, the biblical sinfulness of a private act does not determine whether legislation should be levied to outlaw it.

For the purpose of this discussion, I will stick to the question of public policy. Given the fact that we live in a pluralistic democracy with a spectrum of experiences and deeply held convictions at play, how then shall we live together?

THE END OF DISCRIMINATION

I agree with Tony Campolo, the prolific Evangelical preacher and evangelist who, in 2003, stood in the shadow of the Federal Marriage Amendment and stated in a public debate with his wife, Peggy, a staunch advocate of gay rights, that, "At this particular point we have to agree on one thing: [gay and lesbian people] are entitled to an end to all forms of discrimination. There should be no legal system that gives rights to heterosexual couples that it does not make available to homosexual couples."[147]

Brian Murphy, a filmmaker and web-designer who self-identifies as queer, shared a story with me in a recent interview. A friend of Murphy's attended an Evangelical college and grew up with no gay friends or family. During a classroom discussion of homosexuality and gay rights on solely a conceptual and theoretical level, Murphy's friend had an epiphany: these are people. We're not just talking about a concept or a theory. These are *people*.[148]

That is my starting point: are lesbian, gay, bisexual, and trans-gender people human? If they are human, then they, too, are made in the image of God. If they are made in the image of God, then they, too, in Genesis 1 were given free will—the right to exercise liberty over their bodies and their lives. This right applies even when I disagree with the liberties they take. What's more, the fact that gays and lesbians are made in the image of God endows them with intrinsic value and the same basic rights and protections afforded to any other human being. To legislate anything less is to set up a society that formally declares a certain class of people as less than human.

And that was a central point made by attorneys David Boies (a liberal) and Theodore Olson (a conservative) who succeeded in overturning California's Proposition 8 in 2010. The controversial 2008 Proposition aimed to ban gay marriage throughout the state. In 2010 they joined forces to fight Proposition 8 because they agreed that to ban a certain set of citizens from the fundamental civil right to love and be united with the person of their choice is to create a formal two-class system of citizenship in the United States. This violates the Fourteenth Amendment to the Constitution, which guarantees equal protection of the law for all U.S. citizens.[149]

Legally, marriage is a fundamental right of citizenship protected by the Fourteenth Amendment. In the 1987 case of *Turner v. Safley,* the U.S. Supreme Court struck down a Missouri Department of Corrections regulation that effectively blocked convicted rapists and murderers from being able to marry while in prison. The Court ruled unanimously that the right to marry is such a fundamental right of citizenship that even convicted rapists and murderers cannot have that right impaired or revoked.[150]

Yet, with the passage of the Defense of Marriage Act (DOMA) in 1996, federal legislation formally defined marriage as a union between one man and one woman, effectively banning same-sex marriage and creating a two-class system for the purpose of federal law in the U.S. The Act does not prohibit states from defining marriage on their own terms, but more than 1,138 rights and protections are conferred to U.S. citizens by the federal government upon marriage.[151] LGBT citizens of the United States have no hope of ever receiving even one of these rights or protections in their lifetime—not under current federal law. They are literally and legally second-class citizens. Thus, on February 23, 2011, President Obama declared the Act unconstitutional and instructed the Department of Justice to stop defending the law in court.[152]

Ron Sider, president of Evangelicals for Social Action, makes a compelling argument against same-sex marriage in his *First Things* article,

"Bearing Better Witness." At the heart of his argument is the meaning and purpose of marriage. Sider argues, "The state must promote the best setting in which to nurture the next generation of wholesome citizens." He then references an article by Susan M. Shell, Chair of the Department of Political Science at Boston College, to buttress his argument. In her article, "The Liberal Case Against Gay Marriage," Shell argues that marriages that do not and have no intent to procreate are not marriages. She asks, "Can those who are not even potentially partners in reproduction, and who could never under any circumstances have been so, actually 'marry"? Her answer is no. Whatever else one may want to say positively about the emotional commitment of two men or two women to each other, it is simply not marriage.[153]

Ted Olson, the conservative litigator in California's Proposition 8 Supreme Court case, does not agree with Sider and Shell. He explains in an interview with Bill Moyers, "We have never in this country required an ability or a desire to procreate as a condition to getting married. People who are at 70, 80, 90-years old may get married. People who have no interest in having children can get married." He adds:

The Supreme Court has said that the right to get married is a fundamental individual right. And our opponents say, "Well, the state has an interest in procreation and that's why we allow people to get married." That marriage is for the benefit of the state. Freedom of relationship is for the benefit of the state." We don't believe that in this country. We believe that we created a government, which we gave certain authority to the government. The government doesn't give us liberty; we give the government power to a certain degree to restrict our liberty, but subject to the Bill of Rights.[154]

THE CULTURE WAR

My co-author's position pushes the extreme edge of current discourse about same-sex marriage. He paints a static caricature of real family life and the state of marriage within the U.S. since the founding of our

Union. In his view, the family equals the Christian family. In his view, there is a cultural war being waged against Christian families and their God-given way of passing on the faith from generation to generation. But the truth is institutions of marriage and family have been on an ever-changing journey since the founding of our nation. The institution of marriage is not static. It is dynamic—and as a woman, an African-American woman, I say thankfully so.

Miscegenation laws, introduced in 1691 in the state of Virginia and 1692 in Maryland, prohibited several ethnic minorities from marrying white Americans until 1967. In the same interview with Bill Moyers, David Boies remembers, "When the Supreme Court held that it was unconstitutional to prevent interracial marriages, 64 percent or more of the population of the United States, about two thirds of the population of the United States, believed interracial marriages were wrong. That's a much higher percentage than opposes gay and lesbian marriage in this country today." Olson adds, "When the Supreme Court had made the decision in Loving versus Virginia in 1967, striking down the laws of 17 states that prohibited interracial marriage, now it's only what? 40 years later? 40 years later we think that's inconceivable that Virginia or some other state could prohibit interracial marriage. It's inconceivable."

CHRISTIAN MARRIAGE IS DYNAMIC

Likewise, the truth about the historic institution of marriage and family—even Christian marriage and family—is dynamic. Martin Luther, the leader of the Protestant Reformation declared in 1522:

> If a woman who is fit for marriage has a husband who is not, and she is unable openly to take unto herself another and unwilling, too, to do anything dishonourable since the pope in such a case demands without cause abundant testimony and evidence, she should say to her husband, "Look, my dear husband, you are unable to fulfill your conjugal duty toward me; you have cheated me out of my maidenhood and even imperiled my honour and

> my soul's salvation; in the sight of God there is no real marriage between us. Grant me the privilege of contracting a secret marriage with your brother or closest relative, and you retain the title of husband so that your property will not fall to strangers. Consent to being betrayed voluntarily by me, as you have betrayed me without my consent." It stated further that the husband is obligated to consent to such an arrangement and thus to provide for her the conjugal duty and children, and that if he refuses to do so she should secretly flee from him to some other country and there contract a marriage.[155]

This teaching would be unthinkable in most Protestant Christian churches today, yet Luther is the original architect of our Protestant faith. Similarly, women were seen as property to be bought and sold with dowries until the late 19th century. Not so today. Rape was legal within marriage in the U.S. until the first state, South Dakota, outlawed it in 1975 and the last state, North Carolina, outlawed it in 1993. In the antebellum south, the Christian vow of marriage did nothing to stop the cultural norm of white masters who serial-raped African-American women enslaved by them and many times even the children born of those rapes and using them both as "bed warmers."[156] As a result, the marriage and family structure in the antebellum south was distorted from the start.

The veneer of the historic American marriage and family and the reality of it are two very different things. Marriage in the church and in the United States, its norms and its practices are dynamic—not static. In the harsh light of day, to suggest that Jesus-following Americans should want to "preserve" the "traditional" status and legal norms of marriage in the U.S. reveals either a deep, and sometimes, willful ignorance about the progressive course of marriage in our nation or, worse, a desire to reclaim the "traditional" place of white males in America.

There are consequences to the two-class system that exists right now in the U.S.—the system that recognizes the humanity of some and not of others. First, real families are at risk. They don't represent the veneer of the "traditional" American family, but same-sex families are here. They already exist. As society withholds the 1,138 federal protections provided by legal marriage status, children are being put at risk. In his interview with Bill Moyers, David Boies reflected on an aspect of the Proposition 8 case: "We said we would prove that preventing gays and lesbians from marrying harmed them and harmed their children. And their own experts, the defendant's own experts admitted that."[157] The court ultimately decided: "Retaining the traditional definition of marriage and affording same-sex couples only a separate and differently named family relationship will, as a realistic matter, impose appreciable harm on same-sex couples and their children."[158]

And there is another consequence. In September 22, 2010, Tyler Clementi, a gay freshman at Rutgers University threw himself off the George Washington Bridge after a severe bullying incident on campus. LGBT young people are 3.4 times more likely to attempt suicide than their heterosexual peers.[159] Brian Murphy reflected, "I've heard Christian pastors say, you shouldn't be gay because people kill themselves. People are committing suicide because you're telling them they're going to hell and not giving them a way to live!"

Murphy explained the effects of constant messages communicating to LGBT people that they are less than human: "We're predators and perverts. People internalize that. There are ways to deal with physical violence that comes against us, but spiritual violence kills the soul."[160]

DEHUMANIZATION KILLS

When I asked Murphy if bullying was the core reason for the high LGBT suicide rate, he replied: "It's an oversimplification to say this person bullied this person and so that's why they killed themselves." He explained the unending anguish of LGBT people, "It's like, 'My family kicked me out.' or 'My church thought this was a sin.' or 'I can't get this job I want because of this.' and 'I can't get married' and 'I can't adopt kids' and 'I don't have access to medical treatment that I need.' All these different things make it hard to exist. So, people are just like, 'This is just too much.'" Dehumanization kills people; not only individuals like Tyler Clementi. It is crushing the soul of this class of people who are literally and legally deemed second-class citizens.

Tony Campolo tells the story of a boy named Roger. Roger was gay. He and Campolo went to the same high school in West Philadelphia in the 1950s. Roger would wait when the other boys took their shower after gym class because he was afraid. And when he came out the other boys, including Campolo, were ready with their wet towels. They would whip their towels at his naked body. They thought it was funny. One day, when Campolo wasn't there, five guys cornered Roger in the shower and urinated on him. That night Roger got up around 2 o'clock in the morning and went down into his basement and hanged himself.[161]

Campolo reflects: "And I knew I wasn't a Christian. Oh, I believed all the right things; I was orthodox. I was Evangelical to the core, but I wasn't a Christian, because if I were a Christian, I would have been his friend. I would have stood up for him. I would have defended him. And when they came to pick on him I would have said, "Lay off! This is Roger, my friend."

Personally, President Obama's position has reflected my own for the past few years. I have whole-heartedly supported civil unions, but have been hesitant to support same-sex marriage. But the process of writing this chapter has been a convicting experience. I know a lot of Rogers. I have called them "friend." But truth-be-told I have been happy to close my eyes while society dehumanizes my friends. That is not love. That is not justice. That is not the way of Jesus.

Campolo says, "I hear from my Evangelical friends often: 'We love homosexuals, *but*...' Well the truth is, there can be no 'but'. We love homosexuals, therefore we must stand up for justice for gay and lesbian people, because justice is nothing more than love translated into social policy.

The church and society are still splitting over the rightness or wrongness of homosexual acts. But we can know that we are talking about people—people made in the image of God. And as long as we maintain a dehumanizing legal system that gives fundamental rights and protections to some and not to a class of others, our society is in sin.

THE STRANGER WITHIN YOUR GATES

ON IMMIGRATION

ON IMMIGRATION

LISA SHARON HARPER

"When an alien resides with you in your land, you shall not oppress the alien. The alien who resides with you shall be to you as the citizen among you; you shall love the alien as yourself, for you were aliens in the land of Egypt: I am the Lord your God."

~ Leviticus 19:33-34

"I was a stranger and you welcomed me..."

~ Matthew 25:35b

God's first command to humanity in Genesis 1:28 is, "multiply and fill the earth." In modern terms: "Migrate." The ability to move freely between borders is a basic need of humanity established by God in the beginning. The right to move freely across borders is also a basic human right protected under international law and affirmed by our own treaties. When conditions in one's country of origin threaten the life or livelihood of its citizens, the right of its citizens to migrate freely within and outside of their nation of origin must be protected. In these cases, the right to move reinforces humanity's right to live.

The Bible repeatedly calls for the protection of the immigrant. For example, when God sets up the laws and policies of his people just before bringing them into the Promised Land, He admonishes them: "When an alien resides with you in your land, you shall not oppress the alien. The alien who resides with you shall be to you as the citizen among you; you shall love the alien as yourself, for you were aliens in the land of Egypt: I am the Lord your God" (Leviticus 19:33-34). Likewise, when Jesus tells the story of Judgment Day in Matthew 25, He explains the just ones will stand on his right and the accursed on his left. To the just ones the Son of Man will invite them to enter the Kingdom of God because "When I was a stranger you welcomed me." Jesus' own immigration ethic is one rooted in the value of welcome and hospitality.

Every nation has the right and responsibility to protect its citizens, and in the wake of the terrorist attacks of 9/11 and the current economic recession, the United States has all the more reason to exercise this right and responsibility effectively and efficiently. Yet this is difficult to do when we are faced with an immigration system that is not only faulty, but, indeed, broken.

AMERICA'S SINGLE GREATEST ECONOMIC CRISIS

While the U.S. border is more secure in recent years, the reality is that since 2005, more than 200,000 people each year have crossed our borders without authorization.[162] We don't know who they are. We don't know their backgrounds or intents. We don't know where they're going and we have little means to protect them from predatory employers and human traffickers who exploit vulnerable immigrants for cheap or free labor. In addition, the U.S. unemployment rate is rising; 9.6 percent of Americans were unemployed in October 2010. America is in the throes of its single greatest economic crisis since the Great Depression. We cannot afford the drag on all American wages caused by the exploitation of unauthorized immigrant labor.

That said, consider this: as of January 2009, 10.8 million unauthorized immigrants were residing in the U.S., a decrease of 1.2 million from the previous year. Of the 10.8 million in 2009, only eight percent entered the country since 2005 compared to 28 percent from 2000 to 2004. The last time we saw such a trickle of undocumented immigrants into the U.S. was the period from 1980- 1984. In other words, in the last five years, the flow of unauthorized immigrants into the U.S. has experienced its sharpest decline in 30 years.[163]

Yet, if you watched Fox News in 2010 or listened to Arizona Governor Jan Brewer defend her state's controversial immigration law, SB1070, you likely came away with the impression that illegal aliens are flowing across the borders in greater numbers than ever, taking our jobs, threatening our communities, and even murdering Americans in their sleep. It was an election year.

Here are the facts: at the time Jan Brewer was claiming that every Arizonan had to worry about being beheaded by immigrants hiding in their back yards, violent crimes in Arizona were down by 15 percent since 2006, and the per-capita violent crime rate had dropped by 22 percent in the same period. Not only was the nation as a whole safer than it was three years before, but Arizona was two times safer than the rest of the U.S. Nationally, border cities were among the nation's safest—Phoenix and other large border cities saw crime rates drop by more than 30 percent since the 1990s. And according to Tim Wadsworth, sociologist from the University of Colorado, "Cities with the largest increases in immigration between 1990 and 2000 experienced the largest decreases in homicides and robbery during the same period."[164]

2010 was not the first year in our nation's history that anti- immigrant rhetoric and fear-based legislation were used to stoke the anxieties and prejudices of vulnerable Americans to manipulate votes. Actually this is a tried and true tactic dating back to the 18th century, specifically 1798, when our second President, John Adams, passed the Alien and Sedition Acts to expunge foreigners.

The end of The Civil War in 1865 and the discovery of gold in California in 1848 led to two key legislative landmarks in the 19th Century. The

Fifteenth Amendment was ratified in 1870, granting voting rights to citizens, "regardless of race, color, or previous condition of servitude." In the same year, passage of the Naturalization Act of 1870 granted citizenship to people of African descent after the Civil War. For the first time, the U.S. began to build a framework of citizenship not determined by race and economic status, but rather by the rights, privileges and responsibilities of the citizen. Yet, the residue of racialized politics was not fully rubbed out. The Act explicitly excluded Asians from citizenship.

CHINESE IMMIGRATE TO THE UNITED STATES

With the discovery of gold in 1848, came the first wave of Chinese miners and railroad workers. By 1851, 25,000 Chinese had immigrated to the United States, mostly in and around the gold rush area and San Francisco.[165] In 1852 John Bigler won the re-election as Governor of California calling on the people of his state to "check this tide of Asiatic immigration."

In 1863 the Central Pacific railroad hired Chinese workers and the Union Pacific railroad hired Irish workers to lay the tracks for the first transcontinental railroad. In 1869 the two construction teams laid their last tracks meeting at Promontory Summit in Utah. The railroad was complete. That same year the U.S. ratified the Burlingame Treaty with China, normalizing relations and offering each nation favored-nation status with the other. While citizenship was not offered to Chinese residents, both nations recognized "the inherent and inalienable right of man to change his home and allegiance, and also the mutual advantage of the free migration of their citizens and subjects, respectively for purposes of curiosity, or trade, or as permanent residents."[166]

Yet a series of legislative actions and anti-immigrant movements mounted against the Chinese as early as 1869 when an appeal was made to Congress for legislation to restrict Chinese immigration.[167] By 1870 the Chinese population was 63,199 out of a total U.S. population of 38.5 million and the U.S. was suffering deep economic depression as it struggled to recover from losses on all sides of the Civil War. In addition, big businesses overcapitalized on the railroad industry in 1873 and triggered great panic that left business, railroads, and the Chinese as the chosen targets of American ire. In 1877, Denis Kearney, a major voice of the anti-Chinese movement thundered before his Workingman's Party, "The Chinese laborer is a curse to our land, is degrading to our morals, is a menace to our lives, and should be restricted and forever abolished, and the Chinese must go."[168] Political posturing mixed with brutal opportunism led to the first major law restricting immigration in the U.S.—the Chinese Exclusion Act.

Signed into law on May 6, 1882 by President Chester A. Arthur, the Chinese Exclusion Act halted Chinese immigration for 10 years and officially prohibited Chinese residents from becoming citizens. 1884 amendments clarified that the exclusion applied to ethnic Chinese from any country of origin. Immigration of persons of other races was unlimited during this period. The Act was extended another 10 years in 1892 and became permanent law in 1902 under the 26th President of the United States, Theodore Roosevelt.

Chinese communities felt the law's impact immediately. The law permanently divided families and effectively froze population growth in the Chinese community. Current U.S. residents could not return home to visit their wives and children. Worse still, states like California sought to breed the Chinese out of the U.S. by making it illegal for a Chinese person to marry outside of their race. Since the ratio of men to women at the time of the Act was about 24:1, the Chinese community was effectively frozen.

Today the U.S.' relationship with Mexico with regard to the authorized and unauthorized Mexican immigrants entering the United States is set on a similar trajectory as the Chinese of the 19th century. Like the Burlingame Treaty of 1868, the North American Free Trade Agreement (NAFTA) Treaty, which went into effect in 1994, established favored relations between the U.S., Mexico, and Canada. In an effort to eliminate barriers to trade and investment between North American nations, the treaty phased out tariffs on exports and imports between the U.S., Mexico, and Canada. With bi- partisan support and participation[169], NAFTA negotiations began under the Reagan administration.

THE SEARCH FOR EMPLOYMENT

Corn production has been central to the Mexican economy for centuries, yet U.S. government corn subsidies for U.S. farmers, which totaled $10.1 billion in 2000, are wrecking havoc on the livelihoods of Mexican corn farmers and Mexico's food security.[170] Mexican farmers can't compete with the under-priced corn in the U.S., so they largely have chosen to immigrate from rural to urban areas of Mexico in search of employment. This has placed added burden on Mexico's urban infrastructure and an already frayed poverty safety net.[171]

Plus, Mexico sends nearly 80 percent of its exports to the U.S. In economic boon years, this works as its engineers intended. The strong buying power of the U.S. serves to strengthen the economic standing of Mexico. In recent years, though, the economic crisis in the U.S. has proven the opposite to be as true. As American buying power fell, it took down the Mexican economy with it. A 2009 Congressional Report on U.S.-Mexico Relations reported that the U.S. recession caused the Mexican economy to contract by approximately seven percent, "the worst decline in six decades."[172]

The U.S. economic crisis of 2008 and its subsequent recession have stoked a firestorm of nativist sentiment and legislation similar to the anti-Chinese rants of Denis Kearney and his Workingman's Party. Now the ranters and the legislators are one and the same. Arizona Governor Jan Brewer turned to the registered hate group Federation for American Immigrant Reform (F.A.I.R.) to pen Arizona law SB1070, which effectively expands immigration enforcement jurisdiction from federal to local agencies. The law's components also make citizen and non-citizen immigrants more vulnerable to the infringement of their civil rights through the legalized practice of racial profiling. Twenty other states are following suit—moving to mimic SB1070 even after a Federal District Court stopped the most controversial sections of the law from taking effect.

Comprehensive Immigration Reform (CIR) legislation has been introduced to congress for debate and passage once in the last decade. In 2007 Republican President George W. Bush negotiated CIR legislation that was roundly defeated by his own party when it came to a vote in the Senate. Bush sought to fix our broken immigration system in a way that honored our identity as a nation of immigrants and abided by our high value for hospitality for all. He proposed strong border enforcement as well as an earned path to citizenship for the more than 11 million unauthorized immigrants living within the U.S. at the time. His party plainly dismissed the legislation with one word—"Amnesty."

In April 2010 Senators Charles Schumer (D-NY), Robert Menendez (D-NJ), and Senate Majority Leader Harry Reid (D-NV) introduced an outline for Comprehensive Immigration Reform. Their plan was largely the same as President Bush's, with additional measures to secure the U.S. border and crack down on unscrupulous employers who take advantage of unauthorized workers. The Schumer, Menendez, Reid outline also offered an earned path to citizenship for unauthorized immigrants; requiring all unauthorized immigrants to learn English, pass a background check, and pay a financial penalty for the years of taxes they owe. The Kearneyesque Tea Party fanned the flames of American nativism in mid-2010 and forced the Senate to table immigration reform until after the 2010 mid-term elections.

Consider this: According to a study released by UCLA professor, Dr. Raúl Hinojosa-Ojeda, the U.S. Government has only three options when it comes to immigration reform: 1) Comprehensive immigration reform that creates an earned path to legal citizenship or residence for unauthorized immigrants while making our border more secure, 2) Temporary workers program only—a program that offers temporary worker status to all unauthorized immigrants and future immigrants, and 3) Mass deportation of all unauthorized immigrants and effectively close the U.S.-Mexico border to all future immigration. If the U.S. enacts option 1, Comprehensive Immigration Reform, it will add $1.5 trillion to the U.S. Gross Domestic Product (GDP) over the next ten years. If the U.S. enacts option 2, the Temporary Worker Program, the U.S. only would add $792 billion to the GDP over 10 years. If the U.S. enacts option 3, Mass Deportation, it will cost the nation $2.6 trillion over 10 years.[173] Likewise, the conservative CATO Institute says option 1 would raise the average family income by a total of $300-500 billion over the course of 10 years. These increases are achieved by cracking down on unscrupulous employers who take advantage of unauthorized immigrants, thus raising the wages for all American workers.

THE LIMITATIONS OF INDIVIDUAL LIBERTIES

The United States of America faces a choice as it considers how it will fix its broken immigration system in the 21st century. Will U.S. voters allow themselves to be led by firestorms fueled by recycled fears—fears of the other, fears of loss of money and control, fears that lead to race-based bullying? Or will we be led by faith—faith in our declared values, faith in our immigrant identity, faith in the God who identifies himself as the great protector, faith in Jesus who identifies with the immigrant?

Evangelical Christians must consider that, biblically, fear is the opposite of faith. Fear compels its subjects to take matters into their own hands rather than placing their concerns into the hands of God. Fear compels us to question God's sovereignty and intentions toward us. Fear leads to the oppression and exploitation of people made in the image of God. The phrase "Do not fear" appears 365 times in scripture. Accordingly, Jesus exhorts his followers in Matthew 6:25- 33:

> Therefore I tell you, *do not worry* about your life, what you will eat or what you will drink, or about your body, what you will wear. Is not life more than food and the body more than cloth-

> ing? Look at the birds of the air; they neither sow nor reap nor gather into barns, and yet your heavenly Father feeds them. Are you not of more value than they? And can any of you by worrying add a single hour to your span of life? And why do you worry about clothing? Consider the lilies of the field, how they grow, they neither toil nor spin, yet I tell you, even Solomon in all his glory was not clothed like one of the these. But if God so clothes the grass of the field, which is alive today and tomorrow is thrown into the oven, will He not much more clothe you—you of little faith? Therefore *do not worry*, saying "What will we eat?" or "What will we drink?" or "What will we wear? For it is the Gentiles who strive for all these things; and indeed your heavenly Father knows that you need all these things. But strive first for the Kingdom of God and his righteousness, and all these things will be given to you as well.

If fear is the opposite of faith, then what would faith do? Faith would compel us to trust God and God's ways. It would recognize all of humanity's basic need and right to move freely between borders, especially in cases where the right to migrate reinforces the right to live. It would press us toward the ways of welcome, generosity, and liberty for all. It would call us to seek first the Kingdom of God knowing that as we do so protection, resources, and security will be added unto us. Faith would compel us to value the well-being of all above the comfort of a few. Faith would compel Evangelical voters to support solutions that protect American interests *and* uphold our most basic Christian values.

D.C. INNES

The immigrant's life is my life. In 1958 my parents left Scotland for Canada. They were newly married and had nothing but $300 and a suitcase. It was not quite Ellis Island. My parents were from working class Aberdeen, but my father arrived with a master's degree in behavioral psychology and a government job.[174] My own immigrant story is similar in a way. I didn't show up "homeless and tempest- tossed." I came here for graduate school on a student visa and then, several visas later, qualified for a green card after I married an American. I finally became a citizen in February 2010.[175] Nonetheless, I lived as an alien in this land for twenty-five years, and took no small pains to stay "in status" and legal.

YAY IMMIGRATION!

People across the political spectrum agree that immigration is good for America. Immigration has been fundamental to the country's great success. In large part, our historically open-armed immigration policy explains this. We welcomed Germans and Poles, Chinese and Japanese, Irish and Italians, Cubans and Mexicans, and Africans who came under fundamentally different circumstances. Granted, though we received them, we did not always welcome them. The transition at times was tense, as Lisa demonstrates in her account of the Chinese experience.

At the same time, America has not dissolved into a cauldron of transplanted tribal conflicts. The reason for this is that immigrants here have embraced the principles that have united the disparate peoples of this nation from the time of its inception. Norman Asing is a fine example. He was the Chinese restaurateur in San Francisco who opposed California Governor John Bigler's 1852 campaign against "this tide of Asiatic immigration." In protest, he wrote, "I am a Chinaman, a republican, and a lover of free institutions; am much attached to the principles of the government of the United States...."[176] Asing embraced what he found here while enhancing it by what he brought. In fact, more native born Americans should be just like him. Anyone who opposes immigration itself does not understand America, and so cannot be a patriot in the full.

IMMIGRATION AND ILLEGAL IMMIGRATION

On the whole, the American public favors a generous immigration policy.[177] For years, polls have registered consistently high public support (60 percent) for allowing anyone to join us except "national security threats, criminals and those who would come here to live off our welfare system."[178] But while Americans are generally happy to welcome people who arrive by legal procedures and for legitimate purposes, illegal entry draws a sharply different response.[179] It offends our commitment to equality. Equality demands equality before the law, that everyone obey the same rules and not skip the line.

THE CHRISTIAN VIEW: WELCOMING AND ITS LIMITS

A welcoming attitude toward immigrants is, in a sense, also a Christian position. The Kingdom of God itself is built on immigration of sorts. The Kingdom is a Hebrew kingdom, but its gates have been welcoming Gentiles since Christ gave the Great Commission for his people to disciple the nations. God prepared Israel for this eventuality. As Lisa points out, when the Israelites emerged from Egypt, God's law commanded Israel to be welcoming and kind to the stranger—the sojourner and the immigrant (Leviticus 19:33-34). But if sojourners had numbered in the millions, Israel would have been obviously justified in restricting the influx if nothing else to preserve the nation's character and laws.[180]

We cannot simply reduce the command regarding aliens to a shadow of the gospel in the Old Testament. It is certainly that. But it also contains a principle of moral righteousness. There is a way to treat strangers and wayfarers that is pleasing to God. But all things are to be done decently and in order. It is right to welcome immigrants—those fleeing persecution or simply seeking to enjoy the just fruit of their labors. But given modern means of communication and transportation, open borders could bring a billion people to our shores within a generation. With that level of immigration, America would no longer be America, and that would be everyone's loss. A combination of crime and the old-world political culture of corruption would displace our republic of laws, and liberty would perish. Every ne'r-do-well, from the slumdog pickpocket to the international gangster, knows an opportunity when he sees it.

A hospitable person will welcome others into his home, especially those in need. But it does not follow that he should remove the lock from his door, and let anyone and everyone use his home as a flop house and a rec room. That would be a disservice to everyone, especially to his own family who has first claim on his provision and protection.

ECONOMICS INDICATE A BROKEN SYSTEM

Lisa is correct when she writes that government has a right to control the flow of people into the country for security, to protect U.S. labor, and also to protect the migrants themselves. However, a thriving market in undocumented foreign labor, such as we have, shows that the country's immigration system is woefully inadequate to our labor needs. Put simply, when the economy grows faster than the labor supply, we need immigrants to make up the difference. When the immigration system restricts the influx of labor to a level far short of what the economy needs, people find their way here illegally in search of the unfilled jobs. You might call it the physics of liberty. Lisa points out that "in the last five years the flow of unauthorized immigrants into the U.S. has experienced its sharpest decline in 30 years." The reason for this has to be in large part the economic downturn, especially in home construction. But that means we need to fix the system now in anticipation of renewed pressures when the economy recovers.

THE SOLUTION

Lisa and I more or less agree on the alternatives we face as a nation.

(1) Round 'em up and ship 'em back. But that is practically impossible, and if attempted would likely create more evils than it would remedy. (2) General amnesty. But this is unacceptable for three reasons. There is no political support for it, it would undermine the credibility of our laws (what credibility is left), and it would encourage another 12 million to take their chances for the next amnesty. (3) Some sort of regularization of status with consequences, along with effectively enhanced border security. (Lisa doesn't mention the general amnesty, but does mention a temporary worker program, which I see as part of a regularization of status package.)

Two conservative Evangelicals recently called on our national leaders to attend to justice in sorting out this mess. Mathew Staver, dean of the Liberty University law school and chairman the Liberty Council, insists that the first step has to be credibly securing our borders.[181] Not that we close our borders, but simply that we regain control over who's entering the country, and that we do this for the sake of national security and domestic tranquility—protect American citizens against violent criminals and drug traffickers. This is the basic, biblical function of government. If our government is not securing us against foreign intruders, it is failing in an essential responsibility.

A credible commitment to enforcing existing immigration laws is every bit as much a starting point. Failure in precisely this led the Arizona government to take the controversial step of using state police to enforce federal law. The question should not even arise. The federal government needs to prosecute everyone who knowingly employs undocumented aliens. Biblically, that is the government's job—to make laws for specific and limited purposes and enforce them. What is true of private persons is true also of governments: their yes should be yes, and their no should be no. A law enacted should be a law enforced. Otherwise, far from upholding the laws, government undermines them, encouraging people to ignore what they should scrupulously observe.

Staver admits that one reason so many illegal aliens are in the country is that we have sent a mixed message by our lax enforcement. "We have a 'Now Hiring' sign alongside a 'Keep Out' sign." Can you wink at people who are illegally crossing the border in search of work and then get upset at them and call them criminals once they are here? If our government itself does not take the law seriously, how can we blame people for taking the same view who are just looking work in the land of opportunity? Because of intentionally lax border enforcement (the promised fence is still far from complete), our own government has been complicit in making illegal entry attractive.

Richard Land, president of the Ethics and Religious Liberty Commission of the Southern Baptist Convention, echoed this concern for equity in our treatment of those who are in the country illegally. "[I]t is manifestly unfair to not enforce a law for more than two decades and then all of a sudden announce, now we are going to enforce retroactively laws that have been dormant in terms of enforcement." He brought his point home, adding, "For example, suppose the federal government sent out a notice saying, 'we have been monitoring your habitual exceeding of the speed limits on our interstates over the past 20 years. Now we have the technology to ticket you for each incidence of speeding over the last 20 years. You will be billed retroactively for 20 years worth of speeding tickets.' Does anyone think most Americans would find this either fair or acceptable? I think not."[182]

Amnesty disrespects the law and mass deportation is impractical. Therefore, earned legal status, whether temporary or permanent, is the only remaining option. This would involve, according to Staver, "appropriate penalties, waiting periods, background checks, evidence of moral character, a commitment to full participation in American society through an understanding of the English language, an understanding and affirmation of the rights and duties of citizens and the structure of America's government, and the embrace of American values." Staver stands squarely in the American and Christian tradition of ordered liberty and neighborly compassion when he calls this "a rational and just immigration policy which acknowledges that we are both a nation of immigrants and a nation of laws." This approach upholds the two biblical principles that rightly govern this issue: the rule of law (Romans 13) and kindness to foreigners living among us (Lev. 19), i.e., security and charity.

FINAL THOUGHTS

So if there is so much agreement on the problem and the solution, where is the disagreement in this chapter?

Most of Lisa's argument addresses our history of "anti-immigrant rhetoric and fear-based legislation" such as the Alien and Sedition Acts of 1798, the Naturalization Act of 1870, and the Chinese Exclusion Act of 1882. Those laws go back at least a century, but she presents them as a background for understanding the Arizona law authorizing the co-operative enforcement of federal immigration law.[183] Both houses of the Arizona legislature and the governor are Republican. Whatever the problems or virtues of the law, it's a state law and doesn't directly pertain to the national debate.

Lisa gets to that debate near the end of her chapter where she discusses Comprehensive Immigration Reform (CIR). But there she presents President George W. Bush and the Democrats on the side of all things just and reasonable, and the Republican Party uniformly on the side of xenophobic nativism, a racist obstacle to the only righteous solution to the problem. There were some who, in their understandable concern for the rule of law, smelled amnesty for illegals in the major proposals before Congress. But the controversy for most people was this. Which step was to come first: effective border security or regularization of status for the 11 million people now in the country illegally? Complicating the question was, first, Democrat insistence that effective border security measures come later, raising suspicions that, for partisan electoral reasons, they would never come through on the promise, and, second, a recent history of strengthened border security "on paper only."

If Republicans are to some degree politically motivated in their concerns not to give our 11 million illegal aliens easy access to citizenship (i.e., they will vote largely Democratic), the reverse must also be true. Democrats are in part politically motivated in their concern to provide easy naturalization for these undocumented millions in the hope they will...vote Democratic! So are Republicans putting partisan political concerns ahead of humanitarian ones, or do the Democrats prefer partisan political advantage over the integrity of our laws and our electoral system? If both are true, which is worse? Does it matter which is worse?

The illegal immigration question comes down to these three principles: rule of law, equity in its application, and provision for our national prosperity. Concern for these principles is both Christian and classically republican.

THE WAY OF PEACE

ON WAR AND TERRORISM

ON WAR AND TERRORISM

D.C. INNES

"National security policy" sounds dry and academic to most people. When they hear the phrase "war on terror," however, their interest awakens. When hostile foreign nationals fly planes into American buildings, people see that the political strategy of anticipating and managing foreign conflict is no mere academic concern.

For this reason, the apostle Paul was wise to instruct Timothy that Christians should pray for all those in authority, especially those in the highest authority, so that, as they do their divinely appointed jobs, we would be free to live quiet and peaceful lives in godliness and dignity (1 Tim. 2:2). If government is wicked or incompetent in its stewardship of the national security, the church cannot go about its business as God has called it to do.

THE GENERAL THREAT FROM ABROAD

James Madison wrote in *The Federalist Papers* No. 51, "If men were angels, no government would be necessary." In other words, the sinful nature of man is the chief reason we have government. In political terms, this translates as man's proclivity toward violating his neighbor for selfish gain and his ultimate desire to be absolute master of all things. This is a problem in domestic political life, but the threat is many times greater when it comes from armed invaders.

The domestic arena, while certainly a challenge, is different in nature and more manageable than the international one because the home sphere is under one sovereign power. The sovereign's laws govern it. The sovereign's arm enforces those laws with dread punishment if necessary. There is no force within the domestic realm that can withstand the sovereign political authority. In America, that sovereign is the people acting through the state.

But the international sphere is one of relative anarchy. There is no world government; no single voice speaks laws into existence for every nation, tribe, and tongue. No single arm extends a sword across every ocean and mountain, across every fruited and blighted plain.

True, there are international conventions, protocols, agreements, and treaties, but they have only as much force as nations allow them to have. Their power to bind is political, not legal. What we call "rogue nations," like North Korea and Iran, can flout international standards with impunity, because, being rogues, they are shameless. The United States can refuse to be involved in an international treaty if we think it is hostile to our national interests. As for the United Nations, it is not a government. It can punish only with frowns and scolding. It's a sheath without a sword, a purse without coin, judgment without authority.

For this reason, the community of nations is an especially dangerous place. Specifically, the danger lies in what is all too often the convergence of depravity, ability, and ambition in national leaders whom we call "tyrants." They are a scourge to their own people, but they are also a menace to their neighbors as their ambition is rarely satisfied within their own borders.

Because of this international expression of human iniquity, God has provided armed government not only to punish evildoers at home, but also to repel them from abroad. God authorizes the sword, the power over life and death, because there are cruel beasts at the city gates who will not depart unless they are either destroyed or credibly threatened with destruction. If we were inclined to forget this grisly fact of life, then the events of 9/11 and the atrocities and near atrocities that have punctuated this last decade have helped us keep it in mind.

A wise government, therefore, addresses the task of preserving national security by first understanding human nature and how it behaves under conditions of international conflict. Jesus did not even trust his fans, "because He knew all people and needed no one to bear witness about man, for He himself knew what was in man" (John 2:24-25).

THE PRESENT DANGER

In the twentieth century, Nazi Germany and the Soviet Union were the chief threats to our national security. But the twenty-first century has brought yet another existential threat, this time from a different continent and of a different nature: al-Qaeda and their imitators. In a way, they present a more difficult adversary. They are "non-state actors," and thus a more amorphous opponent. So they are harder to hit. They are also harder, and perhaps impossible, to engage diplomatically.

Their political ideology further complicates the confrontation because it's a form of one of the world's major religions. For this reason, we have found it difficult to name the enemy. We call it variously radical Islam, Islamism, Islamo-fascism, or Jihadism, and sometimes just "terrorism" or "violent extremism."

The blend of politics and religion also makes it difficult for many to identify the nature of the struggle. President Bush declared a "War on Terror," avoiding reference to the beliefs that drive these particular terrorists. President Obama has pulled back even further, choosing to see only a domestic law enforcement issue.[184] So the question is: from a biblical perspective and given this new threat, do the Republicans or the Democrats have a better understanding of human nature, and which party applies it more prudently in dealing with these declared enemies from which God clearly wants people kept safe by their governments?

TWO APPROACHES TO FOREIGN POLICY

Are people basically good and generous or evil and selfish? Are they basically rational or passionate? Different answers produce different foreign policies. The parties do not divide evenly on these questions, but the Democrats tend to be more trusting of foreign leaders to do the right thing when faced with good will on our part. Accordingly, Democrats tend to be more internationalist—more inclined to work through international bodies, more sensitive to international opinion, more trusting in the sufficiency of treaty agreements.

The Republicans, by contrast, tend to be more unilateralist. They are more likely to see international organizations and international opinion as driven by foreign national interests and personal ambitions that can be hostile to what is best for American security and prosperity, perhaps irreconcilably. They are more likely to suffer the world's ill opinion when they are convinced a policy is in our country's best interests. And they are more likely to back up treaties with prudently calculated incentives and disincentives, including credible threats.

That said, however, both parties pursue diplomatic solutions to international conflicts, both parties work through the United Nations, both parties are prepared to use military force, and both parties are concerned about America's moral standing in the world.

But Democrats and Republicans divide broadly between idealism and realism, dovishness and hawkishness, internationalism and unilateralism as default positions. Those who temperamentally or philosophically incline toward the former positions (idealism, dovishness, internationalism) are more trusting of human beings based on a more optimistic view of human nature, whereas those who incline to the latter positions (realism, hawkishness, unilateralism or national self-reliance) are more skeptical of foreign actors based on what I believe is a more biblically justified assessment of what to expect from fallen people in positions of power who are unconstrained by law.

So a fundamental question to ask when assessing candidates for public office is, do they take human depravity in the world seriously? Are they prepared to deal with sin on a political level with all the tools, both rational and coercive, that God has provided? Where a political leader stands on these questions has grave implications for how he will address our twenty-first century terror threat.

THE TWO PARTIES IN DEFENSE OF THE NATION

Since the end of the Vietnam War, the Democratic Party has been fairly consistent in its approach to dealing with threats from abroad. Democrats have been largely naïve regarding what national security requires of us. Their moral expectations regarding other nations, even the most brutal ones, have too often been unjustifiably optimistic.

History shows this repeatedly. The Democratic Congress prematurely cut off funds for South Vietnam after the conclusion of hostilities there, allowing Communist North Vietnamese forces to sweep into the south, forcing our humiliating withdrawal from the embassy rooftop in 1975.[185]

Democratic President Jimmy Carter allowed the Soviet Union to take him completely by surprise with their invasion of Afghanistan. Carter confessed, it "made a more dramatic change in my opinion of what the Soviets' ultimate goals are than anything they've done in the previous time I've been in office." According to two prominent political scientists, "No president in the postwar era has testified more dramatically to his own naiveté."[186]

The next Democratic President, Bill Clinton, came to office completely focused on domestic policy, with little interest in foreign affairs and a discomfort with things military.[187] In the course of his presidency he intervened militarily in Somalia, Haiti, Bosnia, and Kosovo, but in none of these regions were American strategic interests involved. Clinton shared the thinking of today's Democrats, which in foreign policy means, according to Charles Krauthammer, "only humanitarian interventionism—disinterested interventionism devoid of national interest—is morally pristine enough to justify the use of force."[188]

In 2007, Democrats in Congress, including then Senator Barack Obama, publicly declared defeat in Iraq and called for immediate troop withdrawal. Senate Majority Leader, Harry Reid, declared, "this war is lost."[189] This was three months after President Bush announced the so-called "surge," his new counter-insurgency Iraq strategy with significantly higher troop levels.

In office, President Obama has followed the Democratic tendency toward appeasement of hostile powers abroad. Though he is vigorously prosecuting the war in Afghanistan with a troop build-up and predator drones and successfully brought Osama bin Laden his just deserts, he has refused to recognize the nature of the broader conflict—an assault from radical Islamists intent on imposing Muslim Sharia law internationally—and what is necessary to prevail in the struggle.[190]

Obama has been treating the al-Qaeda attacks not as a war but as a domestic law enforcement issue. In the 2008 campaign, he promised to close the Guantanamo Bay Detention Camp, end military tribunals for terror suspects, and put all the detainees into the federal prison and court system.[191] The administration read Omar Faruq Abdulmutallab, the Christmas Day underwear bomber, his Miranda rights as though he were a local gangster.[192] Obama pushed to get Khalid Sheikh Mohammed, the architect of 9/11, tried in federal court in New York City. Political realities have constrained his ability to fulfill these plans, however.[193]

Just as Democrats were appalled by Reagan's description of our communist adversary as an "Evil Empire" twenty-five years ago, today Obama forbids the State Department to use the word "terrorist" for fear of giving offense overseas.[194] Testifying before a Congressional committee, his Attorney General, Eric Holder, would not admit that Islamic religion had anything to do with motivating the failed Times Square bomber.[195] In his remarks at the memorial service for those slain in the Fort Hood shooting spree, President Obama called Mjr. Nidal Hasan's behavior "incomprehensible," even though this obvious terrorist was shouting "Allahu Akbar" (God is great) while he did it.[196] No one can deal effectively with an enemy the nature of whose evil he refuses to face.

The model for Republican foreign policy is still Ronald Reagan, and Republicans continue to judge their leaders by the standard he set. Americans remember him fondly as one of the greatest presidents of the twentieth century and for good reason. Reagan followed a policy of "peace through strength."

In international affairs, policies of weakness embolden evil. President Nixon and his Secretary of State, Henry Kissinger, conceded a large measure of victory to the Soviet Union with a policy of détente. As a consequence, the Soviets through their proxies expanded their influence aggressively in Africa, Central America, and central Asia, most notably in Afghanistan. By contrast, Reagan resolved to name the evil, confront it militarily and diplomatically, and ultimately defeat it. To do this, however, Reagan had to battle not only the East Bloc, but also the timid, concessionist Democratic majority in Congress.

Republican presidents have been far from simple unilateralists, however. Reagan worked within NATO, successfully holding that alliance together even as the Soviets strained to break it apart. His Republican successor in office, George H. W. Bush, assembled a coalition of thirty-four nations to expel Saddam Hussein's Iraqi army from Kuwait in 1991. A decade later, Bush's son, George W. Bush, mobilized American might to disarm Saddam of what the Iraqi dictator led us to believe were weapons of mass destruction. But he first pursued Iraqi compliance with UN sanctions[197] and, having failed in that, assembled a coalition of 30 nations to support the United States in disarming Iraq.[198]

Nonetheless, when defense of the nation has required decisive action, Republican presidents have been far more willing to dispense with extended negotiations and deploy American forces unilaterally.

President Reagan sent troops into Grenada to free American medical students being held by extreme left radicals under Moscow and Fidel Castro's sway.[199] He ordered an air strike against Libya after Muammar al-Gaddafi's agents killed two and injured 79 American servicemen in a West Berlin discotheque bombing. Though America was not alone in the 1991 liberation of Kuwait, George H. W. Bush did not allow himself to be held captive to an extended process of negotiation, which would have given Saddam the opportunity to dig in. After the 9/11 attacks, George W. Bush struck at al-Qaeda and the Taliban in Afghanistan without delay. When the weight of evidence indicated Saddam Hussein had weapons of mass destruction, as well as the motive and means to use them against us, Bush moved swiftly and forcefully to remove the threat after securing a reasonable consensus at home and abroad.

Since the terrorist attacks of September 11, 2001, al-Qaeda has shown itself to be monstrously ruthless and patiently cunning. The horrific events of that day, however, are like a roadside bomb compared to what our Jihadist enemies could inflict if we are not properly vigilant. Consider the slaughter and suffering, as well as economic devastation, that a nuclear or biological bomb in New York City would bring upon us. Love of neighbor requires a tough-minded foreign policy.

This War on Terror requires a clear definition of what that conflict is, who it is we are fighting, why we are fighting, and what we need to do to prevail in the fight. Neither party as a whole has been up to this task. It is profoundly complex and uniquely challenging. However, I find that those who have spoken most soberly and prudently have been at the conservative end of the political spectrum. The GOP has been far more willing to recognize and do what is required to confront and defeat this brutality. They are more ready not to, as the Apostle Paul says, "bear the sword in vain" (Romans 13:4).

LISA SHARON HARPER

"Blessed are the meek, for they will inherit the earth."

~ Matthew 5:5

"Put your sword back into its place; for all who take the sword will perish by the sword."

~ Matthew 26:52

It was 8:30 a.m. in Los Angeles. My apartment mate, Donna, banged on my door, ran into my room, and woke me up out of a deep sleep yelling, "The World Trade Center is gone and America is at war!"

I shot up and ran into the living room where Peter Jennings was explaining that between 8:45 a.m. and 9:05 a.m. eastern time, two airplanes had flown directly into the North and South Towers of the World Trade Center. My roommate and I stood in our Los Angeles living room watching the hour's-old, looped video as Jennings recounted the terror New Yorkers had been experiencing for nearly three hours. We watched the video of the North Tower burning and a second plane hitting the Center's South Tower.

What ensued over the next minutes, days, and years after the two planes hit the towers, is well documented. The images are seared into the memories of all who watched coordinated horrors and our responses to them unfold. A third plane struck The Pentagon at 9:37 a.m. EDT. At 9:59 a.m. the South Tower (Tower 2) buckled and crumbled to earth. At 10:03 a.m.

a fourth flight fell from the sky over Shanksville, Pennsylvania. Finally, at 10:28 a.m., the North Tower disappeared with a crash. Ominous smoke clouds filled with disintegrated steel, concrete, and flesh pushed crazed crowds out of downtown Manhattan and across the iconic Brooklyn Bridge. Airports across the country shut down. No one could get into or out of the United States. And no one knew when or where or if there would be another attack.

2,996 people died that day, including the 19 highjackers who carried out the attacks.

That night, Americans sat stunned and weary from weeping as news channels flashed images of people on every continent wrapped in American flags, mourning in solidarity with us.

The days that followed changed everything.

Thomas Hammarberg, Commissioner for Human Rights at the Council of Europe, has said, "The problem is not whether or not we will react to terrorists, but how?"[200]

How does Jesus respond to terror?

In Jesus' days, the Zealots took up arms to free the Jews of their Roman occupiers and were considered terrorists by the Roman state. In *The War on Terror and the Terror of God*, Lee Griffith notes that in both accounts of the Sermon on the Mount, in Matthew and Luke, "Jesus admonished his followers to turn the other cheek, to love enemies, and to do good to persecutors."[201] Imagine. Simon, the Zealot who believes in the use of violence to fight violence and the poverty caused by Israel's Roman occupation. Jesus had just chosen him to be his follower. Jesus sits him down with the other eleven disciples and begins:

> Blessed are the poor in spirit, for theirs is the kingdom of heaven. Blessed are those who mourn, for they will be comforted.

> Blessed are the meek, for they will inherit the earth. Blessed are those who hunger and thirst for justice, for they will be filled. Blessed are the merciful, for they will receive mercy. Blessed are the *shalom*-makers, for they will be called children of God. Blessed are those who are persecuted for justice's sake, for theirs is the kingdom of heaven. Blessed are you when people revile you and persecute you and utter all kinds of evil against you falsely on my account. Rejoice and be glad, for your reward is great in heaven, for in the same way they persecuted the prophets who were before you. (Matthew 5:3-12)

Griffith illuminates, "The admonitions of the Sermon on the Mount were understood as literal ethical guidance."[202] Jesus demonstrates what it looks like to live according to his own ethical admonitions when He himself is confronted with the Roman Empire's prime instrument of terror—the cross.

Judas betrays Jesus with a kiss in the garden of Gethsemane. A detachment of Roman soldiers along with police from the chief priests and Pharisees moves to seize Jesus. Peter takes out his sword and, in an act of defense, slices off the right ear of a man named Malchus, one of the chief priests' slaves. Jesus says, "Put your sword back into its place; for all who take the sword will perish by the sword." And He touched the slave's ear and it was healed.

Then Jesus stared into the faces of people who considered Him their enemy and He turned his other cheek. He allowed himself to be whipped. He allowed spikes to be driven into his wrists and ankles. He allowed a terrorist state to use his death as a horrifying warning to any who dare follow Him from this point on: declaring allegiance to Jesus will be deemed a direct challenge to the deity of Caesar and to the ultimate authority of occupying Rome. Do so upon pain of death.

Why didn't Jesus fight? After all, that's what the people wanted. They had been waiting for a Messiah to overthrow Caesar by force and take back the Promised Land. Why did Jesus rebuke Peter and heal the slave's ear? Why did He choose the route of silent, non-violent resistance with Pilate rather than lashing out or arguing his case? Why did Jesus turn the other cheek and exercise meekness, which means disciplined power, in the face of terror?

I believe it was because when He looked into the eyes of the chief priests or their slaves or the Roman soldiers, or even Caesar himself, He saw the image of God. How could Jesus strike down the image of God? He came to redeem and restore the image of God on earth, to set the slaves, and the soldiers, and the priests free from the violent reign of men. He came that Caesar himself might be brought back to life by the dominion of God—a dominion characterized by disciplined power, servant leadership, truth-telling, just dealing, reconciliation and reparation, and above all else, love. Jesus did not fight because He believed in redemption.

Griffith reflects, "Conquest comes through the infliction of suffering. Redemption comes through the Suffering Servant."[203] My co-author stated earlier: "God authorizes the sword, a fearsome weapon of deadly consequence, because there are cruel beasts at the city gates who will not depart unless they are either destroyed or credibly threatened with destruction." I do not see the world that way. Rather than cast myself or my nation on the side of good while those who might come against me are automatically cast as evil, I see the entire world and all relationships in it suffering under the repercussions of the Genesis 3 Fall.

We are all fallen and we all suffer the consequences of the choices we all make to exercise a human's kind of dominion rather than God's kind of dominion. We suffer the consequences of our actions to secure our peace at the expense of the peace of others. Griffith clarifies the key distinction between my paradigm and that of my co-author: "These are sharply contrasting views of the world: a world filled with evil in need of conquest, or a suffering creation groaning for redemption."

Gerald Staberock, the deputy secretary general of the World Organization against Torture in Switzerland, illuminates the effect of ethical dualism inherent in the paradigm of war. "The war paradigm works on an "us vs. them" framework...if you speak in the terms of war, you only have friends and enemies."[204]

The United States is a nation founded on core values. We value the rights of the individual, the protection of the rights of minorities, the rule of law, free and fair elections, and due process. Staberock reflected, in a legal paradigm, you have the law, the courts, time- tested processes, and you protect your values. In a war paradigm all bets are off. Individual liberties are severely limited or sacrificed, minorities are vulnerable to scapegoating, and the rule of law is limited because laws change under the wartime paradigm. For example, killing is forbidden in all circumstances in a legal paradigm. In a war paradigm it is not only excusable, but states are expected to kill "the enemy".

Nine days after the tragedy of 9/11, President George W. Bush declared a "Global War on Terror." He named al Qaeda as the terrorist organization responsible for the 9/11 attacks and he drew sharp distinction between our international friends and enemies: "Every nation in every region now has a decision to make: Either you are with us, or you are with the terrorists."[205]

Then on January 29, 2002 in his State of the Union address, the President clarified what came to be known as The Bush Doctrine. With pride our president pointed the finger of judgment at the nations of Korea, Iran, and Iraq and began the war paradigm's process of dehumanization of "the enemy." He named them the Axis of Evil, saying, "States like these and their terrorist allies, constitute an Axis of Evil arming to threaten the peace of the world. By seeking weapons of mass destruction, these regimes pose a grave and growing danger."[206]

The President mentioned ominous characteristics of Korean and Iranian governance, but he spent the bulk of his speech laying the foundation for a declaration of war against Iraq. We now know none of these regimes had anything to do with the attacks of 9/11. What's more, though 15 of the 19 highjackers were Saudi Arabian nationals, the nation of Saudi Arabia has never been the target of any 9/11 military response.

THE DECLARATION OF WAR

In addition, according to the global rules of engagement and international law, for the international rules of war to apply, war can only be declared against a state. War cannot legally be declared against an idea, an organization or a network of individuals or organizations. Accordingly, Bush's "global war on terror" is not a real war and the limitations on personal liberties permitted by the war paradigm do not legally apply. No matter. Bush invoked them anyway. He called for severe violations of individual freedoms like wire-tapping U.S. citizens without a warrant, the round up and detainment of *suspected* terrorists and conspirators *without due process*, and the ability to target minority populations through the use of racial and ethnic profiling.

Further, because the war paradigm inherently dehumanizes—obliterating the image of God in the other—Bush's use of the war paradigm led to the adoption of dehumanizing tactics like torture. On May 1, 2011 Osama bin Laden, the leader of al Qaeda, was killed in a raid ordered by President Obama. The raid took place at bin Laden's compound in Abbottabad, Pakistan, a town just north of the capital city of Islamabad. When the news broke that Osama was dead, members of the Bush White House immediately claimed that torture tactics used on their watch led to the capture of Osama bin Laden. Days later John McCain, the top ranking Republican on the Senate Armed Services Committee, refuted these claims in a Washington Post Op-ed. McCain said, "Former attorney general Michael Mukasey recently claimed that 'the intelligence that led to bin Laden … began with a disclosure from Khalid Sheikh Mohammed, who broke like a dam under the pressure of harsh interrogation techniques that included water boarding. He loosed a torrent of information—including eventually the nickname of a trusted courier of bin Laden.' That is false."[207] McCain went on to explain that though Mohammed had been water boarded 183 times, none of the information obtained using those tactics led to the capture of Osama bin Laden. In fact, much of the information garnered was false and led intelligence operatives to waste time on investigations that led to dead ends. The information that led to the capture and death of Osama bin Laden was obtained overseas using standard interrogation tactics. Torture didn't work.

As well, according to the rule of law in the U.S., any evidence obtained while torturing a suspect is automatically inadmissible in the court of law. Thus, the Bush Administration's use of torture at Guantanamo Bay severely jeopardized the legal prosecution of actual 9/11 conspirators.[208] Likewise, Bush's men used torture tactics on enemy combatants captured in Iraq and Afghanistan. According to the international rules of war, torture is illegal in all circumstances. Thus, the use of torture at Abu Ghraib and other war prisons severely damaged the international credibility of the U.S. cause, the legitimacy of the war and any evidence gained while using those tactics. Finally, our use of torture and other dehumanizing tactics reinforced al Qaeda's message to its base and bolstered terrorist recruitment.

WEAPONS OF MASS DESTRUCTION REMAIN TOP PRIORITY

This is not to downplay the danger of weapons of mass destruction landing in the hands of state and non-state terrorists. The threat is real and remains a top priority of democracies around the world. All the more reason the United States' paradigm for engagement must be effective. My co-author argues for a unilateralist approach that dismisses the United States' accountability to the 191 other member states of the United Nations (UN), a body that the United States took a leading role to establish in 1945 in the wake of the chaos of World War II. He argues that international law and human rights law regimes have no mechanisms of enforcement because they have no leader. Not true.

The UN General Assembly intentionally sits in a circle with the center empty because the charter creators believed no single human being could or should be entrusted with leadership of the entire world. Thus, the UN Security Council was created as the primary enforcement body. Together with the International Criminal Court these two bodies have the power to levy global diplomatic, economic, and judicial pressure on states that pose serious threats to other states or to their own citizens. The U.S. holds a permanent seat on the Security Council. The U.S. helped create the UN Charter and much of its language was modeled after our own Declaration of Independence and Constitution. To boot, the UN's international and human rights laws help the world embrace our fundamental value for the rule of law. Thus, the Internationalist approach that my co- author dismisses actually honors and reinforces the values and principles of the American people.

To be sure, these international mechanisms are far from perfect, yet in our interview Staberock said, "Enforcement is difficult, but there is a legal system. We must strengthen it, not weaken it."[209] Of the alternative war paradigm, Staberock warned, "Many of the measures that create the impression that we target a group, ethnic, religious, etc., under general suspicion might be counter-productive." He continued, "However irrational al Qaeda's ideas may look, they, too, have an audience. The important thing for us is not to create a supportive society for these ideas." The final casualty of the war paradigm is the death of self-awareness and space for repentance for past and present international sin. The adage "all is fair in love and war" prevails in the war paradigm. However, when we lose historical perspective we risk applying the wrong solution toward the current problem and we miss opportunities for international repentance, redemption and restoration.

For example, President Bush's "us vs. them" paradigm prevented him from asking the redemptive questions: Why does Iran always show up on the United States' most hated list? And why does Iran hate America so much? In a redemptive paradigm, Bush might have searched the annals of history and found that Iran was once one of the United States' most favored nations—since President Eisenhower's CIA orchestrated the coup of Mossadaq, Iran's populist Prime Minister in 1953, and replaced a sovereign nation's political leader with a puppet regime that bilked the United States for billions in economic and military aid, kept his own people in poverty and suppressed their democratic aspirations for twenty five years—since then...and until the 1978 Islamic Revolution.

Radical elements fill vacuums of power when there are no credible alternatives. There were no credible alternatives in Iran because we supported an oppressive regime. Iran's radical Islamic Revolution led to the installation of the Ayatollah Khomeini, who promised reform through spiritual repentance and Islamic holiness. It led to the capture of American embassy workers shamefully held hostage for 444 days in 1979-1980, and it led to America's gut-level emotional response to the word "Iran" ever since. And if Bush had looked closely enough before declaring his "Axis of Evil" doctrine, he might have seen a rising modern Iranian middle class disillusioned by a stagnant revolution and hungry for the same moderate secular democratic government once aspired to by Mossadaq.[210] He might have seen the seeds of the 2009 secular democratic Iranian uprising. Bush might have forsaken the paradigm of conquest in favor of meek redemption and restored economic relations to bolster Iran's middle class. Maybe.

The American response to the horror of 9/11 was the paradigm of war; conquest not redemption, "us vs. them" and "friends vs. enemies"—not law. One might argue that the terrorists won on 9/11. Terror laid hold of the American soul and, under the guise of strength, America weakened its grip on its fundamental values: due process, the rule of law, protection of the rights of minorities, and the rights of individuals. As a result, we are all less safe today than we were on September 10, 2001.

Neither party's hands are clean with regard to war and our response to terror. Both parties currently vie for the hearts of hawks not doves. To be called a dove in our society has become a political put down. Still, with the exception of its vote to authorize the Iraq war, the Democratic Party has demonstrated more respect for our nation's fundamental values.

President Obama inherited the legal chaos created by Bush's war paradigm and tolerance of torture. In the first years of his presidency, President Obama systematically strengthened our cooperation with and accountability to the United Nations and international and human rights law bodies. Yet, President Obama has a long way to go to live up to his stated value for the rule of law and due process. On May 19, 2011 a 37-year-old Afghan detainee accused of being a member of al Qaeda died in an apparent suicide inside Guantanamo Bay (Gitmo) prison. He was the eighth Gitmo detainee to die in detention since 2002 when the U.S. began using the base to hold detainees.[211] There are still 171 prisoners imprisoned there. To reconcile his promises with his policies President Obama must shut Guantanamo down.

War is not inevitable. We have choices. We can choose the licentiousness of war and terror or the disciplined power of law and the meek redemption of broken international relationships. War does not ultimately save us from evildoers; it transforms the principled into perpetrators. We must do everything within our power to find another way.

DOMINION OVER THE EARTH

ON THE ENVIRONMENT

ON THE ENVIRONMENT

LISA SHARON HARPER

> *"Then God said, 'Let us make humankind in our tselem (image), according to our likeness; and let them have radah (dominion) over the fish of the sea, and over the birds of the air, and over the cattle, and over all the wild animals of the earth, and over every creeping thing that creeps upon the earth."*
>
> *~ Genesis 1:26*

What you think of the words *image* and *dominion* will determine your approach to creation care, climate change, and environmental justice. Previously, I explained how my understanding of governance and liberty is grounded in a biblical concept of *shalom,* the Hebrew word for "peace." We explored the significance that all relationships created by God were declared "very good" at the end of the sixth day. One of those relationships was the one between humanity and the rest of creation. Thus, Genesis chapters 1-3 offers a crucial picture of what it looks like for humans to be in right relationship with the rest of creation and what it takes to pilfer peace.

The Hebrew word for image used in Genesis 1, *tselem*, means representative figure. The word usually referred to kings who saw themselves as representatives of God on earth. The original hearers of Genesis lived in a region of Ancient Mesopotamia where people believed the elements themselves were gods that played the humans like pawns in ruthless games. Humanity was subject to the elements. To powerless people subject to the whims of self-serving gods, the writer of Genesis 1 reveals the truth; we are not pawns! We are God's representative figures! Not only were we created to be free from exploitation and oppression, as explained in earlier, but all humanity actually is endowed with the dignity of queens and kings. In fact, that is what it means to be human!

Then, in the same verse, the fact that we are made in the image of God is grammatically linked with our call to exercise *dominion* (Gen 1:28). The Hebrew word for dominion is *radah* (dominion, to tread down). As God's representative figures, our *dominion* is to bear the likeness of God's *dominion*—not the kind of rule that serves the self by exploiting its subjects or their resources. God's rule is characterized by emphatic love, blessing, provision, and protection. Consider our earlier discussion of the Ten Commandments. (See Liberty and Justice chapter.) God's kind of dominion actively protects the land by offering the land Sabbath rest along with all workers. Under God's dominion all relationships in creation are characterized by love, truth, reciprocity, servanthood, faithfulness, and humility. The relationships between humanity, vegetation, and animals are all declared "forcefully good." They are practicing and experiencing God's *shalom*.

But when we fail to exercise God's kind of dominion; when we rule for our own benefit; exploiting other humans, plundering and pillaging the rest of God's creation—sucking the earth's veins dry—then *shalom* is shattered.

BASIC NEEDS COMPROMISED

And what is the impact? The basic needs of humanity— air, water, food, shelter, and the ability to exercise agency—are compromised. Abdication of our responsibility to exercise God's kind of dominion on earth, whether by governments or corporations, serves to limit and deprive people made in the *image* of God from the opportunity to exercise dominion, to cultivate, steward, and maintain right relationship with the land. It also destroys the very thing God entrusted to us to protect.

In 1805 Lewis and Clark passed through the territory just north of the land we now call Yellowstone National Park, which straddles Wyoming, Utah, and Montana. On their expedition they encountered Cheyenne, Nez Perces, Crow, and Shoshone among other tribes who had lived on that land for approximately 11,000 years. Lewis and Clark didn't venture south to the Yellowstone area, but were welcomed by the Nez Perces. Within twenty five years President Andrew Jackson signed the Indian Removal Act into law. The U.S. Government's customary doctrine of racial separation led to government-sponsored action to remove or obliterate all indigenous tribes to make room for the waves of white settlers fulfilling America's "manifest destiny." [212] By 1855 the indigenous nations of the west were under constant threat from gold miners and land plunderers. From 1855-1873 the Nez Perces ceded more and more land in dirty treaties. And, in 1872, the United States declared a vast swath of Nez Perces, Cheyenne, and Shoshone land "Yellowstone National Park." It was the first national park in the world and it was for the exclusive use of white settlers; not the Indians.[213]

A PROMISE BROKEN

Five years later, in 1877, the U.S. military massacred 80 Nez Perces people in a surprise attack on their camp and pursued the Nez Perces on an ironic chase south through their former stomping grounds—Yellowstone National Park. The Nez Perces interacted with white campers even as they evaded military slaughter. Eventually the Nez Perces turned north and were caught miles from the Canadian border. They had been promised a small plot of land on Lapwai reservation in Idaho, near their original homelands and only miles from Yellowstone National Park. Instead, upon surrender, they were shipped to Fort Leavenworth, Kansas where they were confined as prisoners of war.

The land was cleared of Indians for the benefit of whites. A stream of poachers, miners, and unscrupulous industrialists flooded west and filled the vacuum. As they did, preservationists like John Muir, founder of the Sierra Club, attempted to preserve portions of the land they loved. Muir's solution was federal ownership of more national park lands in the likeness of Yellowstone National Park. In 1903 he accompanied first-term President Theodore Roosevelt on one leg of an eight-week whirlwind tour of the United States. Muir convinced Roosevelt that the only way to preserve the land was through consolidated federal ownership, management, and regulation. On that same tour Roosevelt echoed Muir's philosophy at the construction site of a new Arch at the north entrance of Yellowstone National Park:

> The Yellowstone Park is something unique in the world in so far as I know. This park was created and is now administered for the benefit and enjoyment of the people. The scheme of its preservation is noteworthy in its essential democracy. The only way that the people as a whole can secure to themselves and their children the enjoyment in perpetuity of what the Yellowstone Park has to give is by assuming ownership in the name of the nation and jealously safeguarding and preserving the scenery, the forests, and the wild creatures.[214]

Teddy Roosevelt was the first American president to make conservation of the environment a prime issue of his campaigns and his administration. In 1906 Roosevelt signed a bill that consolidated control of all Yosemite National Park under the ownership, management, and regulation of the federal government. The National Parks Service was established in 1916. The lands' original stewards removed to enforce the doctrine of racial separation[215], the lands' new steward became the federal government "for the benefit and enjoyment of the people"—the white people.

The modern day environmental movement traces its roots back to Muir, Roosevelt, and others who stoked the fires of the National Parks project. Yet, the movement took new form and focus in the aftermath of the effects of the atomic bomb on the land and people of Hiroshima and Nagasaki, Japan. In 1962 Rachel Carson expanded the circle of concern with her landmark treatise, *Silent Spring,* which examined the effects of pesticides and other pollutants on the natural environment. 1972 brought legislative milestones like the Clean Water Act, the Clean Air Act, the Endangered Species Act and the National Environmental Policy Act.

Then in the 1970s and 80s impoverished Native American and African-American communities began to notice that toxic mining and dumping on their lands by deregulated industries were causing elevated levels of cancer and other life-threatening ailments in their communities. In 1987, the United Church of Christ sponsored a study called "Toxic Waste and Race." The study found a one-to-one correlation between the placement of toxic dumping sites and poor communities of color.[216] The Environmental Justice movement was born—a movement of under-resourced communities of color that stood up and declared with one voice that toxic agents could no longer be dumped into their environments.

The American struggle to conserve resources, preserve green space, and regulate industrial waste is now being played out on a global stage with dire consequences. If action is not taken immediately, God's creation will be compromised. Followers of Jesus must decide how we will respond to the phenomenon called "Climate Change."

THE FATE OF TUVALU

The Polynesian island nation of Tuvalu in the South Pacific is the canary in the proverbial mine of climate change. Melting glaciers have caused the global sea level to rise at a rate of 1.7 millimeters per year for the past century, but since 1993 the rate has jumped to about 3 millimeters per year. At that rate, Tuvalu will be under water within about 20 years.[217] On December 19, 2009, at the United Nations Copenhagen Conference on Climate Change, Ian Fry, International Environment Advisor for Tuvalu, spoke on behalf of the 12,373 souls whose families have inhabited Tuvalu for approximately 3000 years: "The science tells us that we must act now and urgently."

The earth's climate patterns have been relatively stable for more than 10,000 years. Increased greenhouse gas emissions from human industrial activity are causing major changes to these otherwise stable patterns. The burning of fossil fuels (especially oil, coal, and natural gas) is the greatest factor contributing to climate change.[218] Pesticides, fertilizers, deforestation, and methane from beef and beef-dairy production account for another 30 percent of all global greenhouse gases, which have formed a blanket over the earth's atmosphere, trapping additional heat and causing global changes in weather patterns. [219]

According to a National Academies report, the Earth's surface temperature is the hottest in our planet's history since at least the year AD 1600, which is as far back as scientists can project.[220] The Earth's average temperature has "risen 1.4 degrees Fahrenheit since the start of the 20th century—with much of this warming occurring in just the last 30 years."[221] The report further explains:

Prior to the Industrial Revolution, the amount of carbon dioxide released to the atmosphere by natural processes was almost exactly in balance with the amount absorbed by plants and other "sinks" on the Earth's surface.[222]

The burning of fossil fuels releases more carbon dioxide into the earth's atmosphere than can be absorbed. If climate change were not connected to human activity then there would not be a clear correlation between 1) the acceleration of the earth's surface temperature, 2) the rising concentration of greenhouse gases in the Earth's atmosphere, and 3) the onset and acceleration of the modern industrial age.

Further, the World Bank states that in 2005, 50 percent of all carbon emissions were emitted by high-income countries, while low-income countries (1.2 billion population) emitted just 2.6 percent of all carbon emissions in the same year. [223]

The average American emits 20 times more carbon than someone from India.[224] If climate change were not caused by human industrial activity then we would not see such a stark correlation between greenhouse gas emission and the wealth, industry, and consumption of a country.

Why is this a matter of faith? Romans 8:19 explains:

> For the creation waits with eager longing for the revealing of the children of God; for the creation was subjected to futility, not of its own will but by the will of the one who subjected it, in hope that the creation itself will be set free from its bondage to decay and will obtain the freedom of the glory of the children of God.

Paul refers to the effects of the first man and woman's choice to trust their own way to fulfillment and peace, not God's way. They consumed the fruit of the tree of which God commanded them not to eat and, as a result, *shalom* was shattered and creation was cursed (Gen. 3:15,17-19). Now, creation groans waiting for the ones who trust God's way to be revealed!

In the U.S., our increasing addiction to coal, oil and natural gas for electricity and transportation has added to the woes of the people of Tuvalu as well as to the most vulnerable in our own nation. In 2006, U.S. fossil fuel combustion accounted for 20 percent of all fossil fuels burned in the entire world.[225] Plus, U.S. carbon emissions from forestry increased by 26 percent from 1990-2007. Together these realities make us the number one carbon and greenhouse gas producer in the world.

The World Health Organization warns, "The overall health effects of a changing climate are likely to be overwhelmingly negative. Climate change affects the fundamental requirements for health – clean air, safe drinking water, sufficient food and secure shelter."[226] The United States is already experiencing water scarcity in certain regions, particularly in the west and southwest. The U.S. State Department projects that water scarcity will affect "a vast range of socioeconomic activities, such as transportation, agriculture, energy production, industrial uses, and other needs, including human consumption."[227] According to the same report, U.S. public health will also be under major threat by 2050. As heat rises, the 50 most populated eastern cities will likely experience a 68 percent increase in Red Ozone Alert days (when the air quality is unhealthy for everyone). This will be particularly hard on poor communities, people with lung problems, children, and seniors.

In biblical terms, climate change is creation's testimony against humanity. We have failed to exercise God's kind of *dominion* over the rest of creation: we have ruled for our own benefit, and have exploited both humanity and land; we have hoarded and over- consumed resources. As a result, *shalom* is shattered. Climate change is God's wake up call to humanity. Liberty is being abused, the image of God is being threatened, and God's creation is being twisted beyond recognition by our ungodly reign.

The great temptation when talking about something as huge as "the environment" or "climate change" is to feel overwhelmed and, as a result, do nothing. Doing nothing is not neutral and its consequences in this case could be dire. There are simple things we can do and guidelines we can follow as individuals, faith communities, business people, and as policy makers.

Faith Leaders for Environmental Justice, located in New York City, is a collaborative, non-partisan group of faith leaders, environmental justice advocates, government representatives, and individuals committed to leveraging the weight of the faith community's moral authority in partnership with communities bearing the weight of the burdens of environmental injustice. Its work has moved faith communities to take up urban farming and has helped to move policy-makers to adopt environmental and food policies that cultivate the image of God in all New Yorkers. People are learning about the issues facing their communities and how they can make small changes to make a big impact.

On an international level, nations around the world watch U.S. elections and its climate change legislative battles to discern how their own nations' fates will fare. In 2009, the U.S. delegation came into the UN Climate Change Conference in Copenhagen with its hands tied. Not only had the U.S. failed to ratify the Kyoto Protocol (a significant global treaty on climate change that required wealthy nations to cut their emissions) but federal climate change legislation had reached a partisan impasse in the U.S. Senate at the time of the Copenhagen conference.

According to an in-depth report in *The New Yorker*, the bi-partisan coalition that had come together to pass the legislation hit an impasse when Senator Lindsay Graham (R-SC) attempted to use the legislation as a way "to boost the nuclear industry and to expand oil drilling." [228] The oil industry gave approximately 70 percent of all donations to Republican candidates and legislators from 2005-2009.[229] The nuclear industry had given the vast majority of its funding to Republicans from 1997 through 2008. Because of the stalemate at home, the U.S. could not bring anything significant to the international negotiations process and no progress was made.

CLIMATE CHANGE LEGISLATION BLOCKED

As it did in Copenhagen, the Republican Party blocked climate change legislation from moving through the Senate in 2010. The legislation called for a "cap and trade" system that would regulate the total amount of emissions by U.S. industries. The bill aimed to reduce U.S. carbon emissions by 80 percent by 2050. It also included cost protection measures for consumers.

But by April 2010, the bi-partisan coalition had negotiated so much of the effective components of the bill away in deals with the oil, nuclear, and natural gas industries that if it had passed, the legislation would have done little to actually decrease greenhouse gas emissions—and may have ultimately increased them. Fox News didn't help when it stoked constituent ire against the bill falsely characterizing it as a "gas tax." And Sen. Harry Reid placated immigration reform activists by announcing the Senate would move on immigration legislation before climate change. Both bills were important and urgent, but in the cold light of day, the reality was the climate bill was ready to drop. No immigration bill had even been drafted. Reid knew he would need the Latino vote in a tough upcoming election. So, he did the deed and we never heard about it again.[230]

The primary forces behind the demise of America's best chance to date for effective climate change legislation were: 1) a massive move to the radical right among an energized Republican base, 2) the Republican Party's primary industry base—the oil, nuclear, and coal industries, which high-jacked the legislation and stripped it of its ability to actually regulate and lower their industry's emissions, 3) the prioritization of money and political power over principal and people. One wonders if our legislators have ever read "Toxic Waste and Race." Have they ever heard of Tuvalu?

In the American story, since the dawn of the industrial age, there have always been people whose primary goal is to gut the earth in pursuit of money and at the expense of all. There have always been those who worked to conserve and preserve land for the majority through tough fights to place legally binding boundaries on industrial evil. And there have always been the Native Americans, the African- Americans and Latinos and the Tuvalus whose backs have borne the heavy burdens of industrial and legislative indifference.

The fight to stop climate change is a unique opportunity for Evangelicals to join forces with legislators and those carrying the heaviest burdens to push for legislation that will help us all. The demise of the legislation in 2010 proves what Jim Wallis of Sojourners says all the time: Washington works in a way that prevents good people from doing "the right thing" unless a social movement rises up and changes the direction of the wind.

What might have happened for the nation of Tuvalu's prospects for survival if, for example, Evangelical Republicans had risen up throughout 2009 and 2010 and lobbied Graham and other Republican Senators, pressing them to do the right thing by the people of Tuvalu and America's urban and rural poor, and seniors, and children, and all Americans, and all humanity who will be severely affected by climate change in our children's lifetime? What if Evangelicals, who are the core of the Republican base, joined forces with other Christians and other people of faith to mount a collective action campaign to boycott companies that fail to back effective climate change legislation? What if Democratic Senators and White House staffers were less concerned with political posing and power plays as they were with principle and the prioritization of people? What if...

D.C. INNES

If global warming exists at all, it may be a big, inescapable black hole of apocalyptic fate. Recent study has shown that even just using the Internet is warming the planet at an alarming rate. According to a CNN report,[231]

- *"every second someone spends browsing a simple web site generates roughly 20 milligrams of* $C0_2$*."*
- *"the manufacturing, use and disposal of information and communications technology generates about two percent of the world's greenhouse gases—similar to the level produced by the entire aviation industry."*

- *"the computer on your desk is contributing to global warming and*
- *... if its electricity comes from a coal power plant it produces as much CO_2 as a sports utility vehicle. Some studies estimate the internet will be producing 20 percent of the world's greenhouse gases in a decade."*

People who are ecologically concerned and climatologically devoted must, upon reading this, feel like young Martin Luther in the confessional, tormented by his inability not to sin. "I sin (produce carbon emissions) every moment of every day; I sin (produce carbon emissions) in thought, word, and deed; I cannot stop sinning (producing carbon emissions)."

Of course, when Luther despaired of his efforts to overcome and correct his sin, he could turn to the Savior: the crucified, risen, and reigning Christ. But crusaders for the earth who find they are inescapably warming the globe whichever way they turn have no choice but suicide and to recommend the same to others. (I do not recommend this.) Short of this, they point us to a stone-aged world of fear and inactivity.

But this vastly underestimates God's provision for us and radically mischaracterizes his calling for us in this world.

CREATION AND DISTINCTLY CHRISTIAN STEWARDSHIP

From the outset, the Bible sets forth the relationship between man and the rest of creation. "Take dominion," God said (Gen.1:26-28). We call this the creation mandate. This dominion over the creation is not the domination of an invading army. It's not rape and pillage. It's the rule of God's image-bearers, his vice-regents. So it's more like wise kingship or royal stewardship, governing the world in God's place with God's character and goals. God made creation for us, and He made us for Himself. We don't live for ourselves and we don't live for the creation. We use the creation in our service to God for His glory.[232]

While Christian environmentalists agree that we are stewards of the earth for God's sake, they often miss or under-appreciate this definitive feature of Christian stewardship. It's not the stewardship of a museum curator, preserving everything just the way we found it, marking everything with a "Do Not Touch" sign. As we read in the parable of the talents, it's more like the stewardship of an investment banker or trust fund manager, one who takes something of value and develops it into something of much greater value (Matt. 25:14-30).

God made man out of the dust of the ground. Man's first home was thus a dusty wasteland. God then created a garden and set the man in it to guard and tend it. But his human calling went far beyond the garden. He was to take dominion of "the earth," the whole world, with the understanding that the dusty wasteland was potentially a fruitful garden, and, with the right application of human creative labor, much more than a garden. By understanding the world, we can bring out God's glory and God's provision for us, everything from iron and olive oil to plastics and penicillin.

The environmentalist, preservationist view of the world makes light of God's bountiful provision for us. It offers the early Native American as a model of human life in harmony with "the environment." But that supposed harmony is actually just an underuse of the world. It's a short and miserable life in stone-aged poverty, tossed and crushed by a cruelly indifferent world. God provides for his people, but He does so in part by making possible the means for us to take dominion over the world instead of being dominated by it. The environmentalist vision is a false gospel that promises a kind of peace, but in reality it's just surrender, and all the degradation that goes with surrender to a merciless enemy.

The American continent is better now than before the Europeans arrived. Cultivated fields are an improvement over endless grasslands. They feed the world, they lower the price of food for the poor, and they add a previously unseen beauty. Today Manhattan Island is a radical improvement over what it was when Peter Minuit bought it from the Lenape Indians for the industrious Dutch. Now it's a center of world-transforming creativity, enterprise, and wealth production that supplies all nations with mercies and glories. (New York is also a center of perversity and moral poison, but that's a separate issue.)

The environmentalist approach to the world has some representation within the Republican Party, such as the pioneering work of President Theodore Roosevelt in establishing the National Parks Service in 1916, and current leaders like John McCain.[233] While the Republican Party is not a Christian party—neither of the two major parties is—its approach to using the world for human benefit, while not faultless, is closer to the Christian approach than the Democratic Party's tendency toward preservationism.

LEAVE IT TO THE EXPERTS

Lisa's thoughts on "the environment" culminate in her concern over global warming, or what the left now calls "climate change." But I question whether there can be a definitively Christian position on climate change any more than there can be a Christian stance on the causes of autism. It is a highly technical question. Most Christian moral pronouncements on technical issues, whether they have to do with climatology, economics, or nuclear defense strategy, only embarrass the faith.

The National Conference of Catholic Bishops ventured far beyond their sphere of competence in the 1980s when they published authoritative statements on the economy and nuclear weapons.[234] Evangelicals stretched the credibility of church leadership when they took strong positions as Christians on the Panama Canal Treaties of 1977 and the New START treaty of 2010.[235] Like global warming, these are technical questions for trained economists and policy analysts who sit under the pastoral teaching of these church leaders.

Marvin Olasky has a helpful six-step approach for classifying levels of biblical objectivity when assessing questions of this sort.[236] He compares it to the six categories of rapids that white-water rafters describe. Class one rapids are so easy that anyone can ride them, and class-six rapids "whisper death." The controversies of life that call for our biblical moral assessment fall by their very nature into the same six categories, ranging from clear to well-nigh impossible.

Class one is an issue on which the Bible has spoken clearly and explicitly either to praise or condemn.

In class two, the biblical position is implicit but nonetheless clear.

Class three is more difficult. You find people on both sides of the issue appealing to Scripture, but a serious and sober study of the Bible brings faithful people to a common conclusion.

Class four departs from simple reliance on the text of Scripture itself, requiring historical experience to help our understanding of the issue.

Class five appeals more broadly to the biblical teaching on human nature. For example, I make a class five argument for a hawkish foreign policy in this book.

Class six is the furthest removed from biblical teaching or any form of evidence comprehensible by most people. It is "navigable only by experts, who might themselves be overturned. On a class-six issue there is no clear biblical position, no historical trail for the discerning to apply, and not much else to mark our path." Whether there is global warming and, if there is, whether it's good or bad and whether it's man-made or natural, fits into the sixth class.

GLOBAL WARMING IN A POLITICAL ATMOSPHERE

Christian global warming alarmists speak as though it's in class two or three. They sound like Paul Krugman, a Nobel prize-winning economist so confident in his understanding of atmospheric science that he called opposition to the cap-and-trade energy bill "treason against the planet."[237]

The high temperature of the rhetoric coming from non-scientists like Paul Krugman and Al Gore is easy to explain. For the last forty years, jeremiads have been thundering from the left, but the particular impending disaster changes every ten years or so. There's an agenda behind theagenda.

When I was in high school in the 1970s, we were taught that our planet faced serious "limits to growth." Earth was said to be alarmingly frail and inadequate to sustain us. Meanwhile, Paul Ehrlich was shouting "population bomb" on a crowded planet. We had to stop having babies and cut way back on our use of natural resources. The consequences of inaction, the experts assured us, would be cataclysmic. It seemed plausible to me. But southern Ontario wasn't overcrowded, and there were no actual signs we were running out of raw materials.

By the 1980s, when I was at university, orthodox alarm had shifted to the nuclear danger. Somehow, America had elected Ronald Reagan as president, and he was waving around nuclear missiles in a zany attempt to scare off the Soviets, which was surely going to bring down on our heads a nuclear war from which the human race would never recover. "The nuclear clock is ticking," went the chorus. "The end is near! Flee from the wrath to come!" But as we know, Reagan proved wiser than his detractors; the decade ended with the peaceful collapse of our Soviet adversary.

For the decade following the end of the Cold War, those most attuned to the great dangers instructed us in the need for broad environmental concern if we were to "save the planet." But it was more of a catechism than a trumpet call. However, the secular millenarians have found a more immediate threat to justify the highest level of social and political alert: global warming. The message is, "Turn or burn!"

So why this need for secularized hellfire preaching? The seventeenth century philosopher, Thomas Hobbes, provides the answer. Hobbes argues that when faced with an intolerable threat—conditions that will make your life "solitary, poor, nasty, brutish, and short"—the only rational course is to surrender up your liberties to an all- powerful government that will secure you in what is most important: your life.

Leftist believers in the succor of big government find this appealing. The trick is finding a terror big enough in this modern age of peace and comfort to panic people into seeking refuge under the shadow of Leviathan, the almighty state, which Hobbes calls "that mortal god to which we owe, under the immortal God, our peace and defense."[238] Earth in the balance is as big as it gets.

Scientists themselves are divided over whether the planet is indeed warming, partly because the research is incomplete and partly on account of the political passions that compromise the discussion. The academic climate is so politicized that researchers are afraid to question the "politically correct" scientific position. When Joanne Simpson, the world's first woman to receive a Ph.D. in meteorology, retired in 2008, she expressed relief that she was finally free to speak "frankly" of her skepticism over the global warming mantra.[239] After Alan Carlin, an EPA veteran with an M.I.T. doctorate, published a report[240] questioning the science behind EPA calls for massive regulation, the Obama administration suppressed his report, banned him from speaking publicly on the subject, and reassigned him to obscurity.[241]

Like the rest of us, scientists are members of political communities with moral and political passions that cloud their selection and assessment of data. The priests in the white lab coats share our human weaknesses, and are tempted as we are.[242]

Global warming hysteria lost a lot of credibility when a team of English researchers was discovered fudging their data to conform their findings to what they felt they ought to be. The Climate Research Unit (CRU) at the University of East Anglia had been a prominent source of the frantic warnings that life on the planet is in mortal danger from carbon emissions. The research is in, sounded the echo, and there's a solid "consensus" in the scientific community. Therefore, the only rational and morally defensible course was to empower governments everywhere to impose severe restrictions not only on manufacturing but also on every aspect of human life. It was our own generation's "fierce urgency of now," as Martin Luther King Jr. put it with far greater justification.

In December 2009, however, computer hackers made public an embarrassing stack of CRU emails and documents that revealed missing and erroneous data, manipulation and suppression of data, and a pattern of groupthink among scientists involved.[243] Yet they and their political allies had been screaming at us to turn our way of life inside out and upside down on the basis of research they claimed was certain.

A CALL TO HUMILITY

As for those of us down here reading whatever snippets of that lofty science flutter down to our level, let's face it: none of us is competent to "consider the science" that goes into affirming or denying global warming.

But if I were to venture an opinion, I would say that I find it interesting that the world underwent a "Little Ice Age" from roughly 1400-1900, in which case it is reasonable that temperatures should be rising.[244] In view of this larger climatological pattern, if we are in a period of global warming, it is part of a natural cycle and really not a problem. "Climate change" is what the earth has always done, and the warming phases are the beneficial up side of it. Things grow. People flourish. The crisis of climate change is not global warming but the cold, hungry death that comes with a global cooling phase.

But what do I know? Lisa and I are just as politicized as the most notorious of the scientific gatekeepers, but with more excuse. We non-scientist policy warriors dabble in the subject and pretend to understand it, but we're not interested in the science itself. Let's be honest. It's the political and moral questions that drive us. The scientific claims on one side of the question or the other either fit our narratives or they don't, and we take sides accordingly as either skeptic or alarmist.

As a Christian, I trust that God has given us a good world with potential for the development of fantastic wealth. He commanded that we undertake that development, and in Christ He gives us the grace to do it charitably, worshipfully, and responsibly. This good world is not a glass ornament that we might accidentally destroy in our unpacking of God's rich provision. We are not capable of destroying it, whether by nuclear weapons or carbon emissions. But if we neglect that provision, we rob God of His glory and ourselves and our neighbors of the good things God has stored up for us.

PUBLISHER'S NOTE

Through the years, the issues of the day will change and our situations will evolve. Sometimes that means taking a new approach and looking at everything in a new way.

While the situations and issues may change, the fact that we should look at everything through the lens of our faith should not change.

The goal of this book is not to give the final word on these complex and controversial topics, but rather to be a conversation starter.

The authors have given us all a lot to think about and a lot to talk about.

This is a conversation that needs to continue in our homes, churches and communities. People of faith must take this seriously in the years to come so that humanity can flourish as God intends.

To converse with the authors and participate in those conversations, join us at leftrightandchrist.com

ENDNOTES

1 Pierre Trudeau served as Prime Minister of Canada from 1968, when I was six years old, until 1984, with only a few months from 1979 to 1980 when the hapless Joe Clark led a Progressive Conservative minority government.

2 George Grant announced this in 1965 (I was just three) in *Lament for a Nation*. British North America had not survived the assaults of the Liberal Party during William Lyon Mackenzie King's twenty-two years as prime minister and the eight years of his successor.

3 According to an account I heard many years later, he was completely unaware of this connection and was quite startled by the suggestion of it.

4 Diefenbaker was the only conservative prime minister between the Great Depression and Brian Mulroney's 1984 romp to head a majority government.

5 Jonathan Kay, "A Disaster for Canada's Human Rights Commission," *National Post*, March 28, 2008.

6 In 1640 three escaped indentured servants were brought before a Virginia court. As penalty for their escape, the court extended the two white servants' terms by four years. As penalty for the black man's escape, the court extended his term to encompass his entire natural life. While the court justified its ruling based on the black man's status as a non-Christian, it was the color of his skin, not his faith status that was immutable. This 1640 ruling planted the seed of race-based slavery in America. Then within one generation in 1662, the Virginia legislative body passed a law with the doctrine of *partus*. Until then, one's status as a free-born English subject was granted based on the legal free status of the father. Borrowed from Roman civil law, *partus* held that the status of a child followed the status of the mother. This policy presented slave-holders who raped enslaved women with a convenient way to confine the evidence of their sin to the slave quarters while absolving them of any legal responsibility to acknowledge or free their children. Likewise, *partus* ensured slave-holders' free-labor force extending race-based slavery beyond the term of an individual's life to encompass all future generations of the mother's line. By 1670 *partus* extended to Carolina.

7 See Charles Marsh, *God's Long Summer: Stories of Faith and Civil Rights,* (Princeton, Princeton UP, 1997).

8 Carol Anderson, *Eyes Off the Prize: The United Nations and the African American Struggle for Human Rights*, 1944-1955, (Cambridge, Cambridge UP, 2003), pp. 4, 124.

9 *Ibid.*, p. 124.

10 Hear the live recording of Hubert Humphrey's 1948 DCN Speech on YouTube: [http://www.youtube.com/watch?v=8nwIdIUVFm4].

11 Sarah McCulloh Lemmon, "The Ideology of the 'Dixiecrat' Movement," *Social Forces* Vol. 30, No. 2 (Dec., 1951), pp. 162-171.

12 For more on my dual-conversion, read the introduction to my book, *Evangelical Does Not Equal Republican...or Democrat* (New York, The New Press, 2008).

13 *Ibid.*, p. 217.

14 Liberty and justice have been pitted against each other in American discourse since the founding of our union. British philosopher Edmund Burke, founder of the modern Conservative movement railed against the French Revolution in his opus, *Reflections on the Revolution in France* (1790). Burke's firm belief in a natural social order shaped by monarchy, aristocracy, and inherited wealth laid the foundations of his philosophy of economic conservatism. Burke's conservatism called for liberty from government rule over personal wealth to preserve hereditary privilege. It also called for the conservation of the social, economic, and political order to preserve hereditary power. Believing in the doctrine of original sin and the utter depravity of humankind, Burke maintained that the masses were inherently evil. For him, each individual's level in society was pre-destined by divine allocation of unequal capacities, merit, and value. He did not believe in the power of systems, structures, or institutions to make things right or wrong. Rather, Burke believed measures to bring equality the very enemy of liberty. Justice for Burke equaled protection of individual liberty and the current social order against the threat of evil and chaos brought by inherently depraved masses.

Thomas Paine, a founding father of the United States and an original lion of the modern liberal movement, penned *The Rights of Man* (1791, 1792) as a direct rebuttal of Burke's *Reflections*. Paine believed all human beings have basic needs that form the foundations for basic human rights. Likewise, a product of the Enlightenment, Paine believed in the basic goodness of humanity, if it were not for corrupting environmental factors and oppressive systems. Thus, *The Rights of Man* trumpets the need of humanity to overcome oppressive systems in order to realize its inherent equality. Observing the gross disparities in wealth and power that led to the French Revolution, Paine rebuked Burke and lifted up the American Revolution as a prime example of the equalizing power of the democratic republican governmental structure over the oppressive structure of monarchy. Justice for Paine equaled the removal of systemic and environmental barriers to individual liberty and equality.

15 Conor Friedersdorf, "Saving the City: An Interview with Brian Anderson," *The Atlantic*, June 1, 2010. Website.

16 Myron Magnet, "GOP Poster Child: Gotham's Revolutionary," *The New York Post*, August 31, 2004.

17 Romans 12:19; Hebrews 10:30; Deuteronomy 32:35.

18 Cara Buckley, "Man is Rescued by Stranger on Subway Tracks," The New York Times, January 3, 2007.

19 Diane Cardwell, "Subway's Rescuer Receives City's Highest Award," *The New York Times*, January 5, 2007. Website.

20 Jen Chung, "State of the Union Props for NYC Subway Hero," *Gothamist*, January 24, 2007. Website.

21 *Congressional Record*, V. 153, Pt. 1, January 4, 2007 to January 17, 2007.

22 Robert Kolker, "This is the Part Where the Superhero Discovers He is Mortal," *New York Maga-*

zine, April 15, 2007. Website.

23 By today's standards, this is such a restricted view of government responsibility, that it may appear libertarian, but it is not. Libertarianism believes in a morally indifferent government. Moral judgments, according to libertarians, are a private matter. But God has clearly called government to "praise those who do good."

24 I argue this more fully in "Netherlands' Tragedy of State Compassion," The *Washington Times*, July 2, 2010. Website.

25 I thank Dr. Gordon Hugenberger at Gordon-Conwell Theological Seminary for this reading of Genesis 2.

26 This notion was first developed by Klaas Schilder in *Christ and Culture* (1947), and later popularized in Henry Van Til's *The Calvinistic Concept of Culture* (1959), and most recently, John Barber's *The Road From Eden* (2008).

27 George Gilder, *Wealth and Poverty* (New York, Basic Books, 1980), p. ix.

28 Job 31:16-23; Ruth 2, Deuteronomy 24:19-22; Matthew 27:57.

29 Speech entitled, "What's Wrong with Politics?," the Conservative Political Centre Lecture, Blackpool, October 11, 1968.

30 Arthur Brooks, *Who Really Cares: America's Charity Divide* (New York: Basic Books, 2007); pp. 77-82.

31 Robert Rector and Rachel Sheffield. "Air Conditioning, Cable TV, and an Xbox: What is Poverty in the United States Today?," heritage.org, July 19, 2011. Website.

32 Daniel Henninger, "The We're-Not-Like-Europe Party," *The Wall Street Journal*, May 13, 2010; Charles Murray, "The Europe Syndrome and the Challenge to American Exceptionalism," *The American*, March 16, 2009.

33 Taken from D.C. Innes, "Netherlands' Tragedy of State Compassion," *The Washington Times,* July 2, 2010.

34 Samuel P. Huntington, *American Politics: the Promise of Disharmony* (Cambridge, MA, Harvard UP, 1981).

35 The Bipartisan Campaign Reform Act of 2002.

36 No Child Left Behind Act of 2001.

37 Medicare Prescription Drug, Improvement, and Modernization Act of 2003.

38 Craig S. Keener, *IVP Bible Background Commentary: New Testament,* (Downers Grove, IL, InterVarsity Press, 1993), p. 267.

39 See Adam Smith's *An Inquiry into the Nature and Causes of the Wealth of Nations* (1776).
40 Philippe Diaz, *The End of Poverty?*, A Cinema Libre Studio Production in association with Robert Schalkenbach Foundation (2008).

41 Neil Irwin, "Economic data don't point to boom times just yet," The Washington Post, April 13, 2010. Website.

42 Peter J. Elmer and Steven A. Seelig, "The Rising Long-Term Trend of Single-Family Mortgage Foreclosure Rates," Federal Deposit Insurance Corporation (FDIC), Washington DC, 1998, p. 2.

43 E. Scott Reckard, "Foreclosures will keep rising through 2010, report says," *The Los Angeles Times*, November 20, 2009. Website.

44 The National Academies: National Academy of Sciences, National Academy of Engineering, Institute of Medicine, National Research Institute, "Understanding and Responding to Climate Change: Highlights of National Academies Reports," (Washington DC, National Academies Press, 2008), p. 7; see also Jeremy Hance, "Corporations become prime driver of deforestation, giving environmentalists clear target"; and Joana Cabello and Tamra Gilbertson, eds., *No REDD! A Reader* (2010), p. 45.

45 Tax Foundation website, "Federal Income Tax Rates History: Income Years 1913 to 2011," January 1, 2011. Website.

46 Sarah Anderson, John Cavanagh, Chuck Collins, Sam Pizzigati, and Mike Lapham, "Executive Excess 2008: How Average Taxpayers Subsidize Runaway Pay." Institute for Policy Studies and United for a Fair Economy, August 25, 2008, p. 19.

47 David R. Francis, "Congress Pecks Away at CEO Pay," *Christian Science Monitor*, April 30, 2007. Website.

48 Sarah Anderson, John Cavanagh, Chuck Collins, Sam Pizzigati, "America's Bailout Barons: Tax Payers, High Finance, and the CEO Pay Bubble," Institute for Policy Studies, September 2009, p. 6.

49 Jerome Guillet, Inteview in Philippe Diaz's *The End of Poverty?*.

50 Aneel Karnani, "The Case Against Corporate Social Responsibility," *The Wall Street Journal*, August 23, 2010. Website.

51 Aneel Karnani, Interview with *The Wall Street Journal Online,* Podcast: http://podcast.mktw.net/wsj/audio/20100818/pod-wsjjrkarnani/pod-wsjjrkarnani.mp3.

52 Clifford Cobb, Interview for Philippe Diaz's *The End of Poverty?*.

53 The Henry Kaiser Family Foundation, "Focus on Health Reform: Impact of Health Reform on Women's Access to Coverage and Care," December 2010, p. 9.

54 Jane Zhang, "Amid fight for life, lupus victim fights for insurance," *The Wall Street Journal*, December 5, 2006. Website.

55 *Ibid.*

56 *Ibid.*

57 *Ibid.*

58 *Ibid.*

59 *Ibid.*

60 The Fourteenth Amendment to the Constitution of the United States guarantees every citizen (born or naturalized in the U.S.) the right to "life, liberty, and property" and to "equal protection of the laws." Article three of the Universal Declaration of Human Rights extends these civil rights beyond the boundary of U.S. citizenship to protect every human being. The Declaration states, "Everyone has the right to life, liberty, and security of person." Article 25 (1) of the Declaration expounds: "Everyone has the right to a standard of living adequate for the health and well-being of himself and of his family, including food, clothing, housing and medical care and necessary social services, and the right to security in the event of unemployment, sickness, disability, widowhood, old age or other lack of livelihood in circumstances beyond his control."

61 The Commonwealth Fund study defined underinsured as anyone experiencing one of three financial indicators: (1) out-of-pocket medical expenses for care amounted to 10 percent of income or more; (2) among low-income adults (below 200 percent of the federal poverty level), medical expenses amounted to at least 5 percent of income; or (3) deductibles equaled or exceeded 5 percent of income.

62 Cathy Schoen, Sara R. Collins, Jennifer L. Kriss and Michelle M. Doty, "How Many Are Underinsured? Trends Among U.S. Adults, 2003 And 2007," *Health Affairs*, 27, no. 4 (2008): w298-w309.

63 David Leonhardt, "Opposition to Health Law is Steeped in Tradition," *The New York Times*, December 15, p. A1.

64 "This Day in Truman History: November 19, 1945, President Truman's Proposed Health Program," Harry S. Truman Library and Museum. Website.

65 Tim Foley, "The Presidents who took us the closest to Universal Healthcare-Part 1," change.org, February 16, 2009. Website.

66 Tim Foley, "The Presidents who took us the closest to Universal Healthcare-Part 2," change.org, February 16, 2009. Website.

67 Ezra Klein, "The Lessons of '94," *The American Prospect*, January 22, 2008. Website.

68 *The New York Times*, "Times Topics: Health Care Reform Overview". Website.

69 *Ibid.* Also, see HealthCare.gov website.

70 "Obama Signs Health Bill," NYTimes.com video: http://video.nytimes.com/video/2010/03/23/us/politics/1247467431610/obama-signs-health- bill.html.

71 Kuyper spoke these words, perhaps his most memorable and powerful, in his 1880 inaugural address at the dedication of the Free University in Amsterdam.

72 "A Move in the Wrong Direction," *The New York Sun*, September 27, 2007. Website.

73 Thomas Sowell makes this same point in "Utopia Versus Freedom," *National Review Online*, August 4, 2009. Website.

74 "Trends in Health Care Costs and Spending," Kaiser Family Foundation, March 2009; p.1.

75 Barney Frank, an establishment Democrat, told Single Payer Action, "[W]e don't have the votes for [a single payer system]. ... I think the best way we're going to get single payer, the only way, is to have a public option and demonstrate the strength of its power." "Barney Frank: Public Option is Best Way to Single Payer," The Heritage Foundation, July 31, 2009. Barack Obama, campaigning in 2007, expressed the same preference. "If you're starting from scratch, then a single-payer system would probably make sense. But we've got all these legacy systems in place, and managing the transition, as well as adjusting the culture to a different system, would be difficult to pull off." Larissa Macfarquhar, "The Conciliator: Where Is Barack Obama Coming From?," *The New Yorker,* May 7, 2007.

76 Kate Devlin, "Sentenced to Death on the NHS," *The Telegraph*, September 2, 2009. Website.

77 Regina Herzlinger, "Why Republicans Should Back Universal Health Care," *The Atlantic*, April 13, 2009. Website.

78 Sarah Palin, "Statement on the Current Health Care Debate," *Facebook,* August 7, 2009. Website.

79 Robert Pear, "Obama Returns to End-of-life Plan That Caused Stir," *The New York Times,* December 25, 2010. Website.

80 Eben Harrell, "How Much is a Year of Life Worth?," *Time*, March 27, 2009. Website.

81 President Obama takes for granted that evaluating the improvements in people's lives as a result of a medical expenditure is a social judgment to be made by government agents. Reflecting on his own grandmother's hip replacement just weeks before her death and after she knew she had cancer, he said "you just get into some very difficult moral issues" when considering whether "to give my grandmother, or everybody else's aging grandparents or parents, a hip replacement when they're terminally ill. ...The chronically ill and those toward the end of their lives are accounting for potentially 80 percent of the total health- care bill out here." Nonetheless, he said he would have paid for it himself if he had to "just because she's my grandmother." Hans Nichols, "Obama Says Grandmother's Hip Replacement Raises Cost Questions," *Bloomberg News,* April 29, 2009.

82 Cal Thomas, "She Told Us So," Worldmag.com, December 30, 2010. Website.

83 "[D]o not be surprised when life-and-death decisions about you or your family are taken out of your hands—and out of the hands of your doctor—and transferred to bureaucrats in Washington." "Utopia Versus Freedom," *National Review Online*, August 4, 2009. Website.

84 D.C. Innes, "Netherlands' Tragedy of State Compassion," *The Washington Times*, July 2, 2010. Website.

85 Jane Zhang, "Amid fight for life, lupus victim fights for insurance," *The Wall Street Journal*, December 5, 2006. Website.

86 George Will, "The Stealth Single-Payer Agenda," *The Washington Post*, June 21, 2009. Website.

87 Cpforlife.org, "What Barack Obama Defended Three Times: Live Birth Abortion," *Free Republic,* August 11, 2008. Website.

88 I say "the baby's" humanity. The different stages of a baby's development have technical terms to identify them—zygote, foetus, etc., and those are legitimate for medical purposes. But in common discourse, a woman refers to her "baby" throughout the process. No unindoctrinated woman suffering a miscarriage would say that she lost her "fetus" eight months into her pregnancy. Unless you want to kill it, convince someone else to kill it, or speak of it with cold, scientific abstraction for some other reason, it's a baby, regardless of its stage of development. When discussing human things, it is proper to use the terms common to ordinary human life. The alternative is to prejudice

the discussion in favor of moral indifference before it even begins.

89 Susan Friend Harding, "The Pro-life Gospel" in *Nothing Sacred: Women Respond to Religious Fundamentalism and Terror,* ed. Betsy Reed (New York, Nation Books, 2002), p.287.

90 Randall Balmer, *Thy Kingdom Come: How the Religious Right Distorts the Faith and Threatens America,* (New York, Basic Books, 2006), p. 16.

91 In 1980, *Moody Monthly*, an influential Evangelical magazine, featured Dr. Koop on the cover holding a baby in an issue intended to introduce Evangelical Christians to abortion as a question on which there can be only one morally serious answer. Dick Bohrer, "Deception on Demand," *Moody Monthly* (May 1980), pp. 24-34.

92 Harding, p.290.

93 Ronald Reagan, "Abortion and the Conscience of the Nation," *National Review Online*, June 10, 2004. Website.

94 Third Bush-Kerry debate, Tempe AZ, Oct 13, 2004.

95 "Obama Lifts Ban on Abortion Funds," *BBC News,* January 24, 2009. Website.

96 Charles Babington, "Stem Cell Bill Get Bush's First Veto," *The Washington Post*, "Vetoes by President George W. Bush," United States Senate.

97 *Human Cloning and Human Dignity: The Report of the President's Council on Bioethics* (New York, Public Affairs, 2002).

98 *Stenberg v. Carhart,* 530 U.S. 914 (2000).

99 *Gonzales v. Carhart,* 550 U.S. 124 (2007).

100 *Planned Parenthood Of Missouri v. Danforth*, 428 U.S. 52 (1976).

101 *Akron v. Akron Center For Reproductive Health*, 462 U.S. 416 (1983). The court upheld limited parental consent for minors after a waiting period in *Hodgson v. Minnesota* (1990).

102 *Planned Parenthood Assn. v. Ashcroft*, 462 U.S. 476 (1983).

103 *Thornburgh v. Amer. Coll. of Obst. & Gyn.,* 476 U.S. 747 (1986). The court upheld a form of informed consent in *Planned Parenthood v. Casey* (1992).

104 Susan Cohen, "Toward Making Abortion 'Rare': The Shifting Battleground over the Means to the End," *Guttmacher Institute* 9, no. 1 (Winter 2006).

105 "Memorandum on Title Ten 'Gag Rule,'" January 22, 1993. The Title X Family Planning program of the Public Health Service Act was enacted in 1970, and is dedicated solely to providing comprehensive family planning and related preventive health services with an emphasis on low income families. "Family Planning," hhs.gov (US Department of Health and Human Services Office of Population Affairs).

106 "Memorandum on the Mexico City Policy," January 22, 1993.

107 "Memorandum on Fetal Tissue Transplantation Research," January 22, 1993.

108 "Memorandum on Abortions in Military Hospitals," January 22, 1993.

109 "Memorandum on Importation of RU-486," January 22, 1993.

110 "Abortion History Timeline," nrlc.org (National Right to Life). Website.

111 Robert George, "Obama's Abortion Extremism," ThePublicDiscourse.com, October 14, 2008. Website.
112 Robert George and Yuval Levin, "Obama and Infanticide," ThePublicDiscourse.com, October 16, 2008. Douglas Johnson and Susan Muskett, "Barack Obama's Actions and Shifting Claims on the Protection of Born-Alive Aborted Infants—and What They Tell Us About His Thinking on Abortion," nrlc.org, August 28, 2008. Website.

113 "Obama and Infanticide," *FactCheck.org*, August 25, 2008. Website.

114 Julie Rovner, "'Partial Birth Abortion:' Separating Fact from Spin," npr.org, February 21, 2006. Website.

115 "Supreme Court Upholds Federal Abortion Ban, Opens Door for Further Restrictions by States," *Guttmacher Policy Review,* Spring 2007, 10:2. Website.

116 Dalia Sussman, "Conditional Support Poll: Thirty Years After *Roe vs. Wade*, American Support Is Conditional," *ABC News,* January 22, 2003. Website.

117 "Abortion in the United States: Statistics and Trends," nrlc.org. Website.

118 See Exodus 20:1-26, 1 Timothy 1:9-10, 1 Corinthians 6:9-10.

119 Norma McCorvey, *Won by Love* (Nashville, Thomas Nelson Publishers, 1997), p. 241.

120 U.S. Supreme Court, *Roe v. Wade*, 410 U.S. 113 (1973), opinion of the Court delivered by Justice Harry Blackmun, Section VIII.

121 *Ibid.*, Section IX.A.

122 *Ibid.*, Section X.

123 Randall Balmer, *Thy Kingdom Come: How the Religious Right Distorts the Faith and Threatens America,* (New York, Basic Books, 2006), p. 12.

124 *Ibid.*, p. 13.

125 *Ibid.*, pp. 13-15.

126 Abortion Surveillance—United States, 2006. Table 2. Morbidity and Mortality Weekly Report, Vol. 58, No. SS-08. Centers for Disease Control and Prevention, November 2009.

127 http://www.pregnantpause.org/lex/partveto.htm.

128 U.S. Supreme Court, *Gonzales v. Carhart*, No. 05-380 (2007), dissenting opinion of the Court Delivered by Justice Ruth Bader Ginsburg.

129 Lawrence B. Finer and Stanley K. Henshaw, "Abortion Incidence and Services in the United States in 2000," *Perspectives on Sexual and Reproductive Health*, Volume 35, Number 1, January/February 2003, The Guttmacher Institute.

130 Rachel K. Jones, Lawrence B. Finer and Susheela Singh, "Characteristics of U.S. Abortion Patients, 2008," Guttmacher Institute (New York, May 2010).

131 *Engel v. Vitale*, 370 U.S. 421 (1962).

132 *Eisenstadt v. Baird*, 405 U.S. 438 (1972).

133 Cal Thomas and Ed Dobson, *Blinded By Might* (Grand Rapids, MI, Zondervan, 1999); pp. 21- 27.

134 "Gay areas are jubilant over Clinton," Jeffrey Schmalz, *The New York Times*, November 25, 1992. Website.

135 "Presidential Proclamation—Lesbian, Gay, Bisexual, and Transgender Pride Month," May 28, 2010. President Obama made similar proclamations in 2009 and 2011.

136 "Obama says his views on same-sex marriage are 'evolving'," Perry Bacon Jr., *The Washington Post*, December 23, 2010. Website.

137 "Obama administration will no longer defend DOMA," Brian Montopoli, *CBS News*, February 23, 2011. Website.

138 "Fox News Poll: Gay Marriage, Immigration, WikiLeaks," Dana Blanton, *Fox News*, August 13, 2010. Website.

139 *Reflections on the Revolution in France* (paragraph 75).

140 Daniel Cere. *The Future of Family Law: Law and the Marriage Crisis in North America* (New York, Institute for American Values, 2005); pp. 7-8, 14-15. These selections discuss the "close relationship" model for marriage.

141 *Ibid.;* pp. 12-14.

142 Incidentally, this has nothing to do with the principle of the separation of church and state. The First Amendment does not require people to set aside their religiously formed moral principles when making the moral judgments that political judgments require. President John Adams (1735-1826) was speaking the common sense of his day when he said, "Our Constitution was made only for a moral and religious people. It is wholly inadequate to the government of any other."

143 "On Family Values," a speech to the Commonwealth Club of California, May 19, 1992. "It doesn't help matters when prime time TV has Murphy Brown—a character who supposedly epitomizes today's intelligent, highly paid, professional woman—mocking the importance of fathers, by bearing a child alone, and calling it just another 'lifestyle choice.'"

144 Barbara Dafoe Whitehead, "Dan Quayle was Right," *Atlantic Magazine,* April 1993. Website.

145 "David Epstein Incest Charges: Columbia Professor Charged with Sleeping with Daughter," The Huffington Post, December 10, 2010; "Columbia Professor is Charged with Incest," Melissa Grace, *New York Daily News*, December 10, 2010 .

146 The Barna Group, "New Marriage and Divorce Statistics Released," March 31, 2008. It is worth noting that only 26 percent of Evangelicals had experienced divorce. Evangelicals qualified as born again, but also met seven other narrowing criteria. Still more than one quarter of all Evangelicals have experienced a divorce, even by Barna's narrow standards.

147 Tony Campolo, audio recording of "Tony and Peggy Campolo Dialogue at the Gay Christian Network Gathering" (2003).

148 Brian Murphy, Transcript of audio-taped interview with author, January 4, 2011, p. 7.

149 David Boies, Transcript of Theodore Olson and David Boies interview on "Bill Moyer's Journal," February 26, 2010.

150 *Turner v. Safley* 482 U.S. 78 (1987).

151 Dayna K. Shah, "Defense of Marriage Act: Update to Prior Report" (2004), United States General Accounting Office, p. 1.

152 Charlie Savage and Sheryl Gay Stolberg, "In Shift, U.S. Says Marriage Act Blocks Gay Rights," *The New York Times,* February 24, p. A1.

153 Ron Sider, "Bearing Better Witness: Evangelicals Need to Rethink what they Do and Say about Gay Marriage," *First Things,* December 2010. Website.

154 Theodore Olsen, Transcript of Theodore Olson and David Boies interview on "Bill Moyer's Journal," February 26, 2010.

155 Martin Luther, "The Estate of Marriage" (1522), Walter I. Brandt, trans.

156 Harriet A. Jacobs, *Incidents in the Life of a Slave Girl: Written by Herself, Jean Fagan Yellin,* ed. (Cambridge, MA, Harvard UP, 1987), pp. 13-14, 18, 27-30, 73-75.

157 Boies, Transcript, p. 17.

158 The Supreme Court of California, In re Marriage Cases, S147999, San Francisco County, JCCP No. 4365, p. 11.

159 Suicide Prevention Resource Center, *Suicide risk and prevention for lesbian, gay, bisexual, and transgender youth.* (Newton, MA, Education Development Center, Inc., 2008). Website.

160 Murphy, Transcript, p. 4.

161 Campolo, audio recording (2003).

162 Michael Hoefer, Nancy Rytina, and Bryan C. Baker, "Estimates of Unauthorized Immigrant Population Residing in the United States January 2009," Department of Homeland Security – Office of Immigration Statistics Report (January 2010).

163 *Ibid.*

164 "Fact Sheet: Setting the Record Straight on Border Crime," *Center for American Progress,* June 14, 2010. Website.

165 "Immigration: The Journey to America – The Chinese," ThinkQuest, Oracle Education Foundation.

166 Hamilton Fish, "Text of the Treaty between China and the United States, Generally known as The Burlingame Treaty of 1868," United States of America Department of State, p. 6.

167 "The Chinese Exclusion Act: Report and Resolutions Adopted for the Chamber of Commerce of the State of New York, December 5, 1889" (New York, 1889) p.11.

168 http://www.thesocialcontract.com/artman2/publish/tsc0603/article_546.shtml.

169 President George H. W. Bush signed NAFTA in 1992 and President Bill Clinton ratified it in 1993.

170 Subsidies are a form of financial assistance, in this case given by the U.S. Government to large farm businesses to help increase the production of corn. In accordance with the rules of supply and demand, subsidized products can be sold at a lower cost because farmers are able to produce more at lower cost to themselves.

171 Rick Relinger, "NAFTA and US Corn Subsidies: Explaining the Displacement of Mexico's Corn Farmers," Prospect: Journal of International Affairs at UCSD, April 2010.

172 Clare Ribando Seelke, "Mexico-U.S. Relations: Issues for Congress," Congressional Research Service, September 2, 2010, p. 7.

173 Dr. Raúl Hinojosa-Ojeda, "Raising the Floor for All American Workers: The Economic Benefits of Comprehensive Immigration Reform," Center for American Progress Immigration Policy Center, January 2010, p. 10.

174 My dad made $4,260 a year and my mom $50 a week. The monthly rent for a small apartment was $98.

175 D.C. Innes, "What I Saw at the Naturalization," *The Washington Times*, March 16, 2010, p. B1.

176 "A Bill Moyers Special: Becoming American—The Chinese Experience. Eyewitness," pbs.org. Website.

177 Incidentally, pollster Scott Rasmussen reports, "Republicans are a bit more supportive than Democrats of a welcoming immigration system." (NRO Symposium, "Appraising Arizona," *National Review Online*, April 28, 2010.) I take the reason for this difference to be the powerful role of trade unions in the Democratic Party. Cheap, non-unionized, immigrant labor threatens union jobs and inflated union-negotiated compensation packages.

178 "58% Say No to Children of Illegal Immigrants," *Rasumussen Reports*, June 3, 2010.

179 "To the political class, the distinction between legal and illegal matters little. To most voters, it matters a lot. In fact, while seven voters out of ten say border enforcement is a higher priority than legalizing undocumented workers, most also favor a welcoming immigration policy." NRO Symposium, "Appraising Arizona," op. cit.

180 For similar reasons, Bermuda has a highly restrictive policy. If they were to throw open their doors, the world's billionaires would flood into their small paradise island, buy up the property, and displace the Bermudians from their own country. The small mountain nation of Switzerland is also particular about who they admit for citizenship. By contrast, several European nations that have had fairly open policies are concerned they might become Muslim majority nations governed by Sharia Law sometime in this century.

181 Testimony before the U.S. House Judiciary Committee's Subcommittee on Immigration, Citizenship, Refugees, Border Security, and International Law, July 14, 2010.

182 *Ibid.*

183 http://azgovernor.gov/dms/upload/SB_1070_Signed.pdf.

184 "Terror Verdict Tests Obama's Strategy on Trials," Charlie Savage, *The New York Times*, November

18, 2010. Website.

185 Stephen E. Ambrose and Douglas G. Brinkley, *Rise to Globalism* (New York, Penguin Books, 1997), pp.243-250.

186 Steven W. Hook and John Spanier, eds., *American Foreign Policy Since World War II,* (Washington, DC, CQPress, 2004); p.179.

187 Joe Klein, *The Natural: The Misunderstood Presidency of Bill Clinton* (New York, Doubleday, 2002); pp.69-71.

188 Charles Krauthammer, "Democratic Realism: An American Foreign Policy for a Unipolar World," American Enterprise Institute, February 10, 2004. Website.

189 Joel Roberts, "Senator Reid on Iraq: 'This War is Lost'," CBS News, April 20, 2007; Jeff Zeleny, "Leading Democrat in Senate Tells Reporters, 'This War is Lost'," *The New York Times*, April 20, 2007.

190 Michael B. Mukasey, "The Waterboarding Trail to bin Laden," *The Wall Street Journal*, May 6, 2011. Website.

191 Ken Millstone, "Obama Makes Plans to Close Guantanamo," *CBS News*, November 14, 2008. Website.

192 "Abdulmutallab in 50 Minutes," *The Wall Street Journal*, January 26, 2010. Website.

193 Richard A. Serrano, "Obama to Resume Military Trials for Guantanamo Detainees," *The Los Angeles Times,* March 8, 2011; Kerry Pickett, "Holder on KSM Trial: I Know Better Than Congress," *The Washington Times*, April 4, 2011. Website.

194 "Interview with Homeland Security Secretary Janet Napolitano: "Away From the Politics of Fear," *Spiegel Online*, March 16, 2009. Website.

195 Stephan Dinan, "Holder Balks at Blaming 'Radical Islam,'" *The Washington Times*, May 14, 2010. Website.

196 "Remarks by the President at Memorial Service at Fort Hood," November 10, 2009; "Muslim Major Screamed 'Allahu Akbar' Before Slaughtering 13 at Ft. Hood," Andy Soltis et al., *The New York Post,* November 16, 2009. Website.

197 United Nations Security Council Resolution 1441, November 8, 2002.

198 Steve Schifferes, "US Names 'Coalition of the Willing'," *BBC News*, Mar. 18, 2003. Website.

199 Peter Schweizer, *Reagan's War* (New York, Doubleday, 2002), pp. 207-210.

200 Gerald Staberock, Skype interview with author, February 3, 2011.

201 Lee Griffith, *The War on Terror and the Terror of God*, (Grand Rapids, MI / Cambridge, U.K., Eerdmans Publishing Company, 2002), p. 23.

202 *Ibid.*

203 *Ibid.*

204 *Ibid.*

205 George W. Bush, "Address to a Joint Session of Congress and the American People," September 20, 2001.

206 George W. Bush, "State of the Union Address," January 29, 2002.

207 John McCain, "Bin Laden's Death and the Debate Over Torture," *The Washington Post*, May 11, 2011.

208 "Accused 9/11 Plotter Kahlid Sheikh Mohammed faces New York Trial," cnn.com, November 13, 2009.

209 Staberock.

210 Vali Nasr, *Forces of Fortune: The Rise of the New Muslim Middle Class and What it will Mean for our World,* (New York, Free Press, 2009), pp. 23-26.

211 The Associated Press, "Lawyer: Gitmo prisoner who died was mentally ill," May 19, 2011. Website.

212 The doctrine of Manifest Destiny was the widely held belief that the United States was ordained by God to expand its territory from coast to coast and to spread its institutions and the inherent virtue of its people throughout the world thereby redeeming the world by making it over in the image of the United States. America's inherent virtue was declared, most notably, by John Winthrop in his sermon, "A City Upon a Hill" (1630).

213 Dee Brown, *Bury My Heart at Wounded Knee: An Indian History of the American West,* (New York, Henry Hold Books, 1970), pp. 316-330.

214 "The National Parks: Americas Best Idea, a film by Ken Burns," pbs.org. Website.

215 Throughout the nineteenth century, court cases that focused on the working relationship between blacks and whites in the public square laid the foundations for the landmark Supreme Court case, *Plessy v. Ferguson* (1896), which transformed the customary Separate but Equal doctrine into U.S. federal case law. The next landmark Supreme Court case, *Brown v. The Board of Education Topeka* (1954) decided that racial separation of children in public schools violates their Fourteenth Amendment right to equal protection under the law. This ruling laid the foundation for the Civil Rights Act of 1964, which effectively ended state-sanctioned segregation in the United States. Though this fight was waged on the stage of black and white relations in the United States, its repercussions have been realized in America's social and systemic dealings with all people of color from the nineteenth century to present day.

216 Robert Bullard, Paul Mohai, Robin Saha, and Beverly Wright, "Toxic Waste and Race Twenty Years Later," United Church of Christ (2007).

217 N.L. Bindoff, J. Willebrand, V. Artale, A, Cazenave, J. Gregory, S. Gulev, K. Hanawa, C. Le Quéré, S. Levitus, Y. Nojiri, C.K. Shum, L.D.Talley and A. Unnikrishnan, "Observations: Oceanic Climate Change and Sea Level. In *Climate Change 2007: The Physical Science Basis. Contribution of Working Group I to the Fourth Assessment Report of the Intergovernmental Panel on Climate Change"* [Solomon, S.,D. Qin, M. Manning, Z. Chen, M. Marquis, K.B. Averyt, M. Tignor and H.L. Miller (eds.)]. (Cambridge, UK, Cambridge UP, 2007), p. 409.

218 The National Academies: National Academy of Sciences, National Academy of Engineering, Institute of Medicine, National Research Institute, "Understanding and Responding to Climate Change: Highlights of National Academies Reports," (Washington DC, National Academies

Press, 2008), p.15.

219 Dipti Thapa and Marjory-Anne Bromhead, "The Hague Conference on Agriculture, Food Security and Climate Change Opportunities and Challenges for a Converging Agenda: Country Examples," (The World Bank, October 2010, Conference Edition), p. 2.

220 The National Academies, p. 5.

221 *Ibid.*, p. 2.

222 *Ibid.*, pp. 5-6.

223 Worldbank.org

224 Eoearth.org

225 United States Department of State, *U.S. Climate Action Report 2010*, (Washington, Global Publishing Services, June 2010), pp. 24-25.

226 *Ibid.*

227 *Ibid.*, p. 88.

228 Ryan Lizza, "As the World Burns: How the Senate and White House missed their best chance to deal with Climate Change," *The New Yorker*, October 11, 2010. Website.

229 Lauren Hepler, "Oil and Gas Contributions Still Rising in 2010 Republicans Receiving Bulk of Industry Cash," OpenSecrets.org. Website.

230 Lizza, "As the World Burns".

231 Lara Farrar, "Greening the Internet," cnn.com, July 13, 2009. Website.

232 The predominant term today for this earthly realm that surrounds us is the environment. The Christian term, however, is "the creation" (Rom. 8:19-22). When thinking about what is true to our faith, Christians should use Christian terminology—the language of Scripture and of the Christian tradition—whenever possible.

233 Hal Bernton, "In Oregon, McCain touts his cap-and-trade system to fight global warming" *The Seattle Times*, May 13, 2008. Website.

234 *Economic Justice for All: Pastoral Letter on Catholic Social Teaching and the U.S. Economy,* November 13, 1986; The Challenge of Peace: God's Promise and Our Response, a Pastoral Letter on War and Peace, May 3, 1983.

235 James Robert Hinkson, *Of Gog and Naboth: The Christian Response to the Panama Canal Treaties of 1977,* M.A. thesis, department of history, University of North Carolina Wilmington, 2006; NAE Press Release: "Evangelicals Concur with Obama on Multiple Issues," December 6, 2010.

236 Marvin Olasky, *Telling the Truth: How to Revitalize Christian Journalism* (Wheaton IL, Crossway Books, 1996); chapter one, "Biblical Objectivity."

237 Paul Krugman, "Betraying the Planet," *The New York Times*, June 28, 2009. Website.

238 Thomas Hobbes, *Leviathan,* C.B. Macpherson, ed. (Harmondsworth, UK, Penguin, 1968), p.227.

239 Kimberley Strassel, "The Climate Change Climate Change," *The Wall Street Journal*, June 26, 2009. Website.

240 Proposed NCEE Comments on Draft Technical Support Document for Endangerment Analysis for Greenhouse Gas Emissions under the Clean Air Act, March 2009.

241 Mike Gonzales, "An Inconvenient Voice: Dr. Alan Carlin," The Heritage Foundation, June 29, 2009. CBS reports on the same story in Declan McCullagh, "EPA May Have suppressed Report Skeptical of Global Warming," June 26, 2009.

242 Thomas Kuhn's *The Structure of Scientific Revolutions* (Chicago, University of Chicago Press, 1962) argued strongly for the "sociology of knowledge," i.e., that scientific inquiry is not in fact separable from the passions, morals, and politics of the scientists.

243 Timothy Lamer, "Cooking Up a Heat Wave," Worldmag.com, December 19, 2009. Website.

244 Viv Forbes, "Climate Change in Perspective," Carbon-sense.com, January 2009; p.4. Prof. Scott Mandia at SUNY Suffolk gives slightly different dates. "Western Europe experienced a general cooling of the climate between the years 1150 and 1460 and a very cold climate between 1560 and 1850 that brought dire consequences to its peoples." He tells us, "One of the worst famines in the seventeenth century occurred in France due to the failed harvest of 1693. Millions of people in France and surrounding countries were killed." In 1816, England experienced "the year without a summer." "The Little Ice Age in Europe."

INDEX BY TOPIC

BY SCRIPTURE

FOR FURTHER READING

ON GOVERNMENT

from LISA SHARON HARPER

Anderson, Carol. *Eyes Off the Prize: The United Nations and the African American Struggle for Human Rights, 1944-1955* (Cambridge UP, 2003).

Brueggemann, Walter. *Peace* (Chalice Press, 2001)

Burke, Edmund. *Reflections on the Revolution in France* (1790)

Galenson, David W. "White Servitude and the Growth of Black Slavery in Colonial America", *The Journal of Economic History*, Vol. 41, No. 1, *The Tasks of Economic History* (Mar., 1981).

Marsh, Charles. *God's Long Summer: Stories of Faith and Civil Rights* (Princeton UP, 1997).

Paine, Thomas. *The Rights of Man* (1791)

Harper, Lisa Sharon with Foreword by Walter Brueggemann. *The Very Good Gospel: How Everything Wrong Can Be Made Right* (Willowbrook, 2016)

from D.C. INNES

Calvin, John. *Institutes of the Christian Religion*, Book IV, chapter 20, "On Civil Government" (1559).

Gerson, Michael, and Peter Wehner. *City of Man: Religion and Politics in a New Era* (Moody Press, 2010).

Goldsworthy, Graeme. *Gospel and Kingdom* (Paternoster Press, 1994). Grudem, Wayne. *Politics According to the Bible* (Zondervan, 2010).

Kuyper, Abraham. "Calvinism and Politics" in *Lectures on Calvinism* (1898).

Wolterstorff, Nicholas. "Theological Foundations for an Evangelical Political Philosophy" in *Toward an Evangelical Public Policy*, Ron Sider and Dianne Knippers, ed. (Baker Books, 2005).

ON BUSINESS

from D.C. INNES

Beisner, E. Calvin. *Prosperity and Poverty: The Compassionate Use of Resources in a World of Scarcity* (Wipf and Stock, 2001).

Gilder, George. *Wealth and Poverty* (Basic Books, 1980).

Innes, D.C. "Netherlands Tragedy of State Compassion," *The Washington Times*, July 2, 2010.

Murray, Charles. *Losing Ground: American Social Policy, 1950-1980* (Basic Books, 1984).

Olasky, Marvin. *The Tragedy of American Compassion* (Crossway Books, 1992).

Tocqueville, Alexis de. *Memoir on Pauperism*, Seymour Drescher, transl. (Ivan R. Dee, 1997).

Wolters, Albert. *Creation Regained: Biblical Basics for a Reformational Worldview, second edition* (Eerdmans, 2005).

from LISA SHARON HARPER

Anderson, Sarah, John Cavanagh, Chuck Collins, Sam Pizzigati. "America's Bailout Barons: Tax Payers, High Finance, and the CEO Pay Bubble," *Institute for Policy Studies*, September 2009.

Cabello, Joana and Tamra Gilbertson, eds. *No REDD! A Reader* (2010).

Diaz, Philippe. "The End of Poverty?", *A Cinema Libre Studio Production* In Association with Robert Schalkenbach Foundation (2008).

Hance, Jeremy. "Corporations become prime driver of deforestation, giving environmentalists clear target", *mongabay.com*, August 5, 2008.

Karnani, Aneel. "The Case Against Corporate Social Responsibility," *The Wall Street Journal*, August 23, 2010.

The National Academies: National Academy of Sciences, National Academy of Engineering, Institute of Medicine, National Research Institute, "Understanding and Responding to Climate Change: Highlights of National Academies Reports" (National Academies Press, Washington DC, 2008).

Schlosser, Eric. *Fast Food Nation* (Houghton Mifflin Company, 2001).

ON HEALTH CARE

from LISA SHARON HARPER

14th Amendment to the Constitution of the United States, The.

Jacobs, Lawrence R. and Theda Skocpol. *Health Care Reform and America Politics: What Everyone Needs to Know* (Oxford UP, October 20, 2010).

Leonhardt, David. "Opposition to Health Law is Steeped in Tradition," *The New York Times*, December 15, pg A1.

The Universal Declaration of Human Rights, Article 3 and Article 25.

The Washington Post, Staff of. Landmark: *America's New Healthcare Law and What It Means for Us All* (Washington Post Public Affairs, April 27, 2010).

from D.C. INNES

Herzlinger, Roberta. *Market-Driven Healthcare: Who Wins, Who Loses in the Transformation of America's Largest Service Industry* (Perseus Books, 1999).

________________. *Who Killed HealthCare?: America's $2 Trillion Medical Problem - and the Consumer-Driven Cure* (McGraw-Hill, 2007).

ON ABORTION

from D.C. INNES

Belz, Mark. *Suffer the Little Children* (Crossway Books, 1989). Hendershott, Anne. *The Politics of Abortion* (Encounter Books, 2006).

Johnson, Abby. *Unplanned: The Dramatic True Story of a Former Planned Parenthood Leader's Journey Across the Life Line* (SaltRiver/Ignatius, 2011).

Nathanson, Bernard. *The Hand of God: A Journey from Death to Life by the Abortion Doctor Who Changed His Mind* (Regnery, 2001).

Olasky, Marvin. *Abortion Rites: a Social History of Abortion in America* (Crossway Books, 1992).

from LISA SHARON HARPER

Balmer, Randall. *Thy Kingdom Come: How the Religious Right Distorts the Faith and Threatens America* (Basic Books, 2007).

Jones, Rachel K., Lawrence B. Finer, and Susheela Singh, "Characteristics of U. S. Abortion Patients, 2008," *Guttmacher Institute* (New York, May 2010).

US. Supreme Court. *Roe v. Wade,* 410 U.S. 113 (1973), Opinion of the Court Delivered by Mr. Justice Harry Blackmun.

U.S. Supreme Court. *Gonzales v. Carhart,* No. 05-380 (2007), Dissenting Opinion of the Court Delivered by Justice Ruth Ginsberg.

ON SAME-SEX MARRIAGE

from D.C. INNES

Cere, Daniel. *The Future of Family Law: Law and the Marriage Crisis in North America, a Report from the Council on Family Law* (Institute for American Values, 2005).

Esolen, Anthony. "A Requiem for Friendship: Why Boys Will Not Be Boys & Other Consequences of the Sexual Revolution," *Touchstone*, September 2005.

"Same-Sex Marriage: Anthony Esolen's Ten Arguments for Sanity," *Touchstone: Mere Comments*, January 25, 2010.

Shell, Susan M. "The Liberal Case Against Gay Marriage," *The Public Interest*, Summer 2004.

Sider, Ron. "Bearing Better Witness," *First Things*, December 2010.

Tubbs, David L. *Freedom's Orphans: Contemporary Liberalism and the Fate of American Children* (Princeton: Princeton UP, 2007).

Tubbs, David L. and Robert P. George, "Redefining Marriage Away," *City Journal*, Summer 2004.

Whitehead, Barbara Dafoe. "Dan Quayle was Right," *Atlantic Magazine*, April 1993.

from LISA SHARON HARPER

Campolo, Tony. audio recording of "Tony and Peggy Campolo Dialogue at the Gay Christian Network Gathering" (2003)

Laycock, Douglas Jr., Anthony Picarello, and Robin Fretwell Wilson. Eds., *Same-Sex Marriage and Religious Liberty: Emerging Conflicts* (Rowman and Littlefield, 2008).

Marin, Andrew. *Love is an Orientation: Elevating the Conversation with the Gay Community* (Downers Grove, IL, InterVarsity Press, 2009).

McLaren, Brian D. *A New Kind of Christianity: Ten Questions that are Transforming the Faith* (Harper Collins, 2010).

Olson, Theodore and David Boies. transcript of interview on "Bill Moyer's Journal," February 26, 2010, *pbs.org*, February 26, 2010.

Suicide Prevention Resource Center, "Suicide risk and prevention for lesbian, gay, bisexual, and transgender youth" (Education Development Center, Inc., 2008).

ON IMMIGRATION

from LISA SHARON HARPER

Burlingame Treaty (1868)

"*The Chinese Exclusion Act: Report and Resolutions Adopted for the Chamber of Commerce of the State of New York*", December 5, 1889" (1889).

de Normandie, Rev. James. "The Injustice to the Chinese" (a sermon preached to the First Church, Eliot Square, Roxbury, November 20, 1892).

Hinojosa-Ojeda, Raúl, Dr. "Raising the Floor for All American Workers: The Economic Benefits of Comprehensive Immigration Reform," *Center for American Progress Immigration Policy Center*, January 2010.

Relinger, Rick. "NAFTA and US Corn Subsidies: Explaining the Displacement of Mexico's Corn Farmers," *Prospect: Journal of International Affairs at UCSD*, April 2010.

Seelke, Clare Ribando. "Mexico-U.S. Relations: Issues for Congress," *Congressional Research Service*, September 2, 2010.

Soerens, Matthew and Jenny Hwang. *Welcoming the Stranger* (InterVarsity Press, 2009).

from D.C. INNES

Tooley, Mark. "Security and Immigration: What is the State's Duty Under God?," *The Review of Faith and International Affairs*, Volume 9: No. 1, March 2011.

ON WAR AND TERRORISM

from D.C. INNES

Bull, Hedley. *The Anarchical Society: A Study of Order in World Politics* (Columbia UP, 1959).

George, Timothy. "Theology for an Age of Terror," *Christianity Today*, September 1, 2006.
Krauthammer, Charles. "Democratic Realism: An American Foreign Policy for a Unipolar World." *The annual Irving Kristol Lecture at the American Enterprise Institute*, February 10, 2004.

Morganthau, Hans. *Politics Among Nations: The Struggle for Power and Peace* (McGraw-Hill, 1948).

Pipes, Daniel. "Distinguishing between Islam and Islamism." A speech delivered at the *Center for Strategic and International Studies* on June 30, 1998.

Pipes, Richard. "Twilight Struggles: the Cold War and the Terror War, alike and not alike." *The National Review*, April 5, 2004.

Schweizer, Peter. *Reagan's War* (Doubleday, 2002).

Scruton, Roger. "The Political Problem of Islam," *The Intercollegiate Review,* Fall 2002.

from LISA SHARON HARPER

The 9/11 Commission Report, (Norton and Company, 2004).

Griffith, Lee. *The War on Terror and the Terror of God,* (Eerdmans, 2002).

Nasr, Vali. *Forces of Fortune: The Rise of the New Muslim Middle Class and What it will Mean for our World* (Free Press, 2009).

ON THE ENVIRONMENT

from LISA SHARON HARPER

Block, Ben. "Interview with Tuvalu Climate Negotiator Ian Fry," *World Watch Institute* website, January 13, 2010.

Brinkley, Douglas. *The Wilderness Warrior: Theodore Roosevelt and the Crusade for America* (Harper Collins, 2009).

Brown, Dee. *Bury My Heart at Wounded Knee: An Indian History of the American West* (Henry Hold Books, 1970).

Carson, Rachel. *Silent Spring* (Houghton Mifflin, 1962).

Hepler, Lauren. "Oil and Gas Contributions Still Rising in 2010 Republicans Receiving Bulk of Industry Cash," *OpenSecrets.org*, October 1, 2010.

Lizza, Ryan. "As the World Burns: How the Senate and White House missed their best chance to deal with Climate Change," *The New Yorker,* October 11, 2010.

The National Academies: National Academy of Sciences, National Academy of Engineering, Institute of Medicine, National Research Institute, "Understanding and Responding to Climate Change: Highlights of National Academies Reports," (National Academies Press, Washington DC, 2008).

NYU Wagner Institute for Civil Infrastructure Systems, "South Bronx Environmental Health Policy Study," October 16, 2006.

United States Civil Rights Act of 1964, (Pub.L. 88-352, 78 Stat. 241, enacted July 2, 1964).

United States Supreme Court. *Plessy v. Ferguson* (1896)

United States Supreme Court. *Brown v. The Board of Education Topek* (1954)

Winthrop, Jonathan. "City on a Hill: A Sermon" (1630)

from D.C. INNES

Beisner, E. Calvin. *Prospects for Growth: A Biblical View of Population, Resources, and the Future* (Crossway Books, 1990).

_________________. *Where Garden Meets Wilderness: Evangelical Entry Into the Enviromental Debate* (Eerdmans, 1997).

Cornwall Alliance. "A Renewed Call to Truth, Prudence, and Protection of the Poor: An Evangelical Examination of the Theology, Science, and Economics of Global Warming" (2009).

Wolters, Albert. *Creation Regained: Biblical Basics for a Reformational Worldview, second edition* (Eerdmans, 2005).

ACKNOWLEDGMENTS

LISA SHARON HARPER

They say it takes a village to raise a child. Books are like authors' children. Authors push out chapters breathing through the agony of the blank page and the blank brain. With each re-write editors, colleagues, and friends "raise" the books through the discipline of red pens and Microsoft's "Track Changes" and "Comments" in the margins. With each reader books are challenged, shaped, and encouraged to reach their full potential. And some very special people are mentors to the author's child just by living their lives and doing what they do. They inspire. It takes a world of influencers, encouragers, challengers and inspirers to raise a book. Then somehow in all the pain, through all the pushing, through all the gentle (and not so gentle) discipline...the book reaches maturity and ventures out to discover life beyond the author's laptop—life in the hands of readers like you.

A true village raised the pages in this book. To them I am indebted. If there be any virtue in the reading, I share the credit with them. If there be any vice, it is because I did not heed their red pens enough. This is the village that raised this book.

Every book needs at least one mid-wife: this one had two. Maritza Crespo and Susan Sharkey witnessed my procrastination, sweaty palms, lack of sleep, anxiety, fear of the chapter being born under the 2000 word limit, fear of hefty 6,000-word tomes that would take weeks to push out. They were there with prayers and encouragement. And finally they reminded me to breathe told me to push—push through the fear.

Ernest and Sharon L. Harper, my parents, offered their living room as sacred space for the birthing of several first drafts. Then they did what proud grandparents do; they sat and listened to me read each chapter out loud! I am grateful for their patience and partnership in engaging the issues and for their useful feedback—among the sharpest and most helpful critiques I received.

Research assistant, Andrew Wilkes, laid the groundwork for research on several key chapters while Vanessa Carter's forays into my writing cave helped reconnect me to the reader through detailed feedback on every first draft.

There were many who helped shape the book's content, sharpening my understanding of issues. This was especially true of Fay Brown, Andrew Bruce, Tony Campolo, Mae Cannon, Matthew Dunbar, Peter Heltzel, Troy Jackson, Andrew Kotliar, Terry LeBlanc, Terry McGonigal, Brian Murphy, Soong-Chan Rah, Gerald Staberock, Andrea Smith, Stephen Tickner, Rabbi Lawrence Troster, Gary Wiley and the cloud of witnesses that informs, nurtures, and holds me accountable on a daily basis. I am obliged to the Sojourners and New York Faith & Justice communities, my Metro Hope Church community, the National Faith & Justice Network, the Evangelicals for Justice network, the New Evangelical Partnership for the Common Good, the Envision network, and the North American Institute for Indigenous Theological Studies. I am grateful for my roots as a staff-worker with Intervarsity Christian Fellowship. My staff partners' love for scripture and skilled biblical study taught me the value and practice of lived theology.

Thanks also to the diverse body of faith leaders who inspire and inform my understanding of the issues as they play themselves out on the ground: Diane Steinman and the New York State Interfaith Network for Immigration Reform; Chung-Wha Hong whose Christian faith compels her power-packed leadership of the New York Immigration Coalition; the Faith Leaders for Environmental Justice and the many heroes of the Environmental Justice movement who have poured into me over the past three years: Peggy Shepard, Charles Calloway, Elizabeth Yeampierre, Anna Vincenti, Alexie Torres Flemming, Sarah Sayeed, Ibrahim Abdul-Matin, Julien Terrell, Cynthia Peabody, Paul DeVries and so many others.

Rev. Jim Wallis read every page, offered generous feedback, and took time out of his overwhelming schedule to pen a powerful foreword. I am so grateful, Jim. You really are the real deal and I am learning from you. And I am indebted to my mentor Dr. Ron Sider who read key chapters and offered generous and loving feedback even though we differ in our approach to some critical issues. And Dr. John M. Perkins is a mentor whose life and story has spoken to me from up close and far away. I pray these pages do justice to the vision of a man who introduced me to the meaning of the word.

Like an expert artisan, Michelle Rapkin's editorial hand chiseled my tome-length treatises into power-packed, concise chapters. Likewise, Mark Russell's talent and faith made this book happen. He was our cheerleader, advocate, referee, and outstanding publisher.

I am grateful for D.C. Innes's generous feedback and humorous emails.

D.C. held no stops in his writing. His voice was clear and authentic and pressed me to adopt a new mantra: "Is that what I really think?" And so, these pages became a true record of what two very different evangelicals really think about a range of issues—at least for now.

And, finally, thank you to the reader for choosing to wrestle with these timely issues and how they intersect with the faith. Your earnest struggle compelled me to think more deeply than ever about the intersection of my faith and the facts. I hope the product serves as a guide on your own journey. I pray yours is a journey toward another way of engaging the public square.

D.C. INNES

How long does it take to write a book? In my case, 49 years. There are many people who shaped me along the way, and who thus had an indirect hand in this book.

My parents gave me liberty to explore the far horizons and supported me in every way.

Clifford Orwin introduced me to the careful reading of great books, and Thomas Pangle and Christopher Bruell trained me further in the art. Robert Vipond, Robert Scigliano, and Robert Faulkner taught me the problematic nobility and goodness of the American regime. Janice Stein and Donald Hafner showed me the complexities of international affairs. Ernest Fortin made graduate school possible for me and introduced me to the prickly theologico-political problem.

Dan Mahoney at Assumption College showed me how political economy is done.

I cannot forget Glyn Owen who first preached the gospel to me, Greg Beale and Gordon Hugenberger who showed me the unity of Scripture as I had never seen it before, Irfon Hughes who directed me to the ministry and showed me the difficulty of that path, and Bill Shishko and Benjamin Miller who have been teaching the professor so he can in turn teach others.

Mickey McLean has been an encouraging and restraining influence at Worldmag.com, and I thank him for allowing me to incorporate material from my column into this work.

Lisa Sharon Harper has sharpened my focus on the Bible's concern for the poor and the government's special protective role for them. Mark Russell has been an encouraging voice throughout the process and a gentle moderator.

At The King's College, I owe a deep debt of thanks to J. Stanley Oakes who hired a pastor-Ph.D. who was looking for re-admittance to academia. He also prompted a more thoughtful appreciation for the three liberties: spiritual, political, and economic. Peter Wood stood by me in my bumpy transition. Marvin Olasky introduced me to this project. I thank Douglas Puffert for his generous encouragement on my economics chapter. Thanks go to Jonathan Clark and Jane Clark for their faithful labors in research and proofreading, as well as to all my students who prompt me to greater labors of service and depths of faith integration, and who are remarkably kind and understanding.

ABOUT THE AUTHORS

LISA SHARON HARPER

Chief Church Engagement Officer, Sojourners

(Speaker/Activist/Author/Award-winning Playwright/Poet)

From Ferguson to New York to Germany, Lisa has been leading trainings and helping mobilize clergy and community leaders around shared values for the common good, with a focus on racial justice. Prior to joining Sojourners, Lisa was the founding executive director of New York Faith & Justice—an organization at the hub of a new ecumenical movement to end poverty in New York City. In that capacity, she helped establish Faith Leaders for Environmental Justice, a citywide collaborative effort of faith leaders committed to leveraging the power of their constituencies and their moral authority in partnership with communities bearing the weight of environmental injustice. She also organized faith leaders to speak out for immigration reform and organized the South Bronx Conversations for Change, a dialogue-to-change project between police and the community.

Harper's faith-rooted approach to advocacy and organizing has activated people across the U.S. and around the world to address structural and political injustice as an outward demonstration of their personal faith.

Asked why she does what she does, Lisa Sharon Harper's answer is clear: "So that the church might be worthy of the moniker 'Bride of Christ'." Through preaching, writing, training, network development, and public witness Ms. Harper engages the church in the work of justice and peacemaking. For example: Ms. Harper helped build the Evangelical Immigration Table from 2011-2013. She fasted for 21 days as a core faster with the 2013 immigration reform Fast for Families, trained and catalyzed evangelicals in St. Louis to engage the 2014 push for justice in Ferguson and did the same in Baltimore in 2015. Harper was recognized in 2015 as one of "50 Powerful Women Religious Leaders to Celebrate on International Women's Day" by the Huffington Post.

She earned her master's in human rights from Columbia University in New York City and is currently in the process of ordination in the Evangelical Covenant Church.

D.C. INNES

Associate Professor of Politics, The King's College

(Professor/Speaker/Author/Columnist)

Since 2005, D.C. Innes has taught politics at The King's College, an Evangelical Christian college in lower Manhattan. He teaches courses in political theory, and has taught American government, American foreign policy, comparative government, and political economy. He earned his doctoral degree at Boston College where he was a student of Robert Faulkner and Ernest Fortin. He did his undergraduate work in political science and philosophy at the University of Toronto. He also has taught at Assumption College, Stonehill College, and Geneva College.

The focus of his research has been the political philosophy of Francis Bacon, in particular the political significance of modern science, and the role of civil religion in Bacon's political project. "Bacon's New Atlantis: The Christian Hope and the Modern Hope" first appeared in *Interpretation: A Journal of Political Philosophy* (1994), and subsequently in *Piety and Humanity: Essays on Religion and Early Modern Political Philosophy*, edited by Douglas Kries (Rowman and Littlefield, 1997). Recently, Innes contributed "Civil Religion as Political Technology in Bacon's New Atlantis" to an anthology of essays, *Civil Religion in Political Thought*, edited by John von Heyking and Ronald Weed (Catholic University of America Press, 2010). His popular writing has appeared in *The Washington Times, The City,* and *AmericanThinker.com*.

Although a busy professor and family man, Innes has spoken outside the classroom on radio, television, and conferences.

Before coming to The King's College, Innes served for several years in the pastoral ministry in Iowa. He earned his M.Div. degree at Reformed

Presbyterian Theological Seminary in Pittsburgh after initial studies at Gordon-Conwell Theological Seminary. He was ordained in the Presbyterian Church in America and is now a minister in the Orthodox Presbyterian Church.

Born and raised in a Scottish-Canadian household, Innes came to the United States for graduate school, and opportunity took him from there. He lives on Long Island with his wife and four children.

ENDORSEMENTS

Left, Right & Christ *couldn't have been written at a better time. Christians are exhausted from the worn out and unbiblical claims that God favors one political party. Harper and Innes have written a fascinating book rooted in biblical truth rather than partisan hackery. They provide a thought-provoking journey through the hot button issues of our day and leave the reader feeling encouraged and informed. I can't wait for their next book!*

KIRSTEN POWERS
Fox News contributor and *Daily Beast* columnist

You might take serious issue with Lisa Sharon Harper's political ideas. You might be frustrated with D.C. Innes' take on American exceptionalism. That's beside the point. What's impressive and important is that in Left, Right & Christ *these two Christians share the platform, and engage in civil dialogue with each other and their readers, in a manner too seldom seen in our public life. Let's hope this book and all it represents are signs of a new era in which Christian faith is not confined to one end of the political spectrum, and in which the application of faith to issues does not start arguments so much as provoke thoughtful, idealistic discussion.*

TOM KRATENMAKER
Contributing religion-in-public-life columnist for *USA TODAY,*
Author of *Onward Christian Athletes*

D.C. Innes and Lisa Sharon Harper are to be commended for their efforts in Left, Right & Christ. *Harper (Left) and Innes (Right) discuss health care, abortion, same sex marriage, immigration, war and peace and the environment from their differing perspectives. Many readers will find as I did that they are often somewhere in between the two authors on many of these issues. However all readers will be informed and challenged by this book."*

RICHARD LAND
President, The Ethics & Religious Liberty Commission
of the Southern Baptist Convention

We live in an age of partisanship and incivility where simple issues have become battlefields for fierce division. In such a moment, American Christians on the left and right must relearn the art of graceful and winsome dialogue. In Left, Right & Christ, *Lisa Sharon Harper and D.C. Innes attempt to build bridges of understanding across the divides on our sharpest disagreements. Read this book, and decide for yourself!*

JONATHAN MERRITT
Author of *A Faith of Our Own: Following Jesus Beyond the Culture Wars*

Left, Right & Christ *is provocative! As one would expect, it provokes readers to think seriously about diverse issues in light of what it means to live as Christians. But I also found it provoked me to ask deeper questions of why some arguments in this book are better than others. It provoked me to pledge to express my own views on these complex subjects with greater care and humility. Finally, this book prompted some great discussions with my wife and teenage daughters. I'm betting it will provoke these much-needed discussions in a variety of contexts.*

THOMAS JAY OORD
Professor of Theology and Philosophy, Northwest Nazarene University
Co-author of *The Best News You Will Ever Hear*

An honest and daring conversation about the toughest political issues facing Christians today. We need to replace the shallow and polarized talking points currently overrunning the public square with thoughtful and nuanced discussion. Left, Right & Christ *is a step forward in that direction. This type of constructive dialog across the political spectrum is both necessary, and* Left, Right & Christ *demonstrates that it is possible.*

BEN LOWE
Author and Activist

I highly recommend this strikingly fresh contribution to the question of how evangelicals should relate to contemporary American politics and public policy. One might have thought there was nothing new to say in or about this burnt-over district, but in their sharp yet civil dialogue, D.C. Innes and Lisa Sharon Harper offer provocative and creative new reflections. One clear takeaway: there is almost no "center" here, but instead at every turn stark clashes in theological, ethical, and political judgment that track closely with similar clashes in the broader American political landscape. I cannot say that this book gives me hope. I can say that it is a high-quality contribution to the conversation.

DR. DAVID P. GUSHEE
Distinguished University Professor of Christian Ethics Director,
Center for Theology and Public Life, Mercer University

Harper and Innes provide one the best examples of the fact that being evangelical comes with no particular political ideology. If you're a serious Christian this book will make you think deeply about why you believe what you believe about social justice.

ANTHONY B. BRADLEY, PhD
Associate Professor of Theology and Ethics, The King's College

Lisa and David take an incredibly brave step with their new book by writing honestly and openly about some of the most hot-button issues of our generation. They debunk the myth that Evangelical Christians have one political perspective and present compelling Bible-based arguments from both sides of the political aisle. Their positions, which are sure to cause some debate in the Christian community, illustrate the complex nature of faith in the public square. Left, Right & Christ *breaks new ground by laying out a substantive and civil debate about our nation's most controversial political issues. For those who seek to understand how people of faith can agree to disagree, I highly recommend this book.*

NICOLE BAKER FULGHAM
Vice President, Faith Community Relations, Teach For America

I am tired of partisanship in both church and society. It seems that we find it impossible to listen and hear one another. Harper and Innes not only represent two different views about the role of government but they represent two very different social and familial backgrounds. This makes for a welcome dialog that will surely benefit fair-minded readers of this well-conceived book.

JOHN H. ARMSTRONG
President, ACT 3, Carol Stream, IL

The vexed question of faith and politics continues to arouse strong feelings among Christians. In this context, it is a pleasure to see the publication of this book by Lisa Sharon Harper and D.C. Innes. A dialogue, a polemic, and a provocative engagement over the issues by two sharp, thoughtful and informed minds from either side of the political spectrum, this book is both entertaining and timely. No one can possibly agree with all that is said here (!), but all should be challenged, provoked and informed by seeing the interchange of ideas it contains. I am grateful to both authors for making me sit up and listen.

CARL TRUEMAN
Professor of Historical Theology and Church History,
Westminster Theological Seminary

NO TREES WERE HARMED IN THE MAKING OF THIS BOOK.

OK, so a few did make the ultimate sacrifice.

In order to steward our environment, we are partnered with *Plant With Purpose,* to plant a tree for every tree that paid the price for the printing of this book.

To learn more, visit www.elevatepub.com/about

CPSIA information can be obtained
at www.ICGtesting.com
Printed in the USA
LVOW04s0539201216
518031LV00008B/189/P